Tuesday Mornings with the Dads

Stories by Fathers Who Have Lost a Son or a Daughter

Foreword by Tony Dungy

PORTLAND • OREGON
INKWATERPRESS.COM

Cover and interior design by Masha Shubin

Cover illustrations
Man © 2009 Robert Redelowski. Image from BigStockPhoto.com
Coffee Cup © 2009 Claudio Baldini. Image from BigStockPhoto.com

www.inkwaterpress.com

ISBN-13 978-1-59299-434-2
ISBN-10 1-59299-434-2

Publisher: Inkwater Press

Printed in the U.S.A.
All paper is acid free and meets all ANSI standards for archival quality paper.

Dedicated to all the fathers of the world

who have lost a son or a daughter

with a special recognition of

JOE LEONARD

who was a part of the Dads Group until

his untimely death on October 16, 2007

Table of Contents

Preface

TWO DADS MET AND SHARED THEIR TRAGIC STORIES WITH EACH OTHER, EACH HAVING LOST A SON.

A THIRD DAD JOINED THEM, HAVING LOST A DAUGHTER.

A FOURTH DAD SHOWED UP, THEN A FIFTH, THEN A SIXTH, UNTIL—MANY MONTHS LATER—THERE WERE SIXTEEN DADS GETTING TOGETHER EACH TUESDAY MORNING AT 7 A.M.

The person who initially connected the first two, and then the third, was Marsha Hutchinson, a second-career seminary student (now an ordained pastor) at St. Luke's United Methodist Church in Indianapolis, Indiana. Without her sensitivity, and without her initiative, there would probably not be a Dads Group. To Marsha we offer our deeply felt thankfulness for her intuitive awareness and her consequential actions.

Those of us in the group have shared our experiences over and over again for more than five years. We know the stories well, especially those of us who have been in the group from its early days. However, our personal experiences with loss and grief are not known by many others except for some family members and close friends.

The idea of sharing our experiences with a wider audience emerged in discussion in late 2007. We agreed we would each have the opportunity to write our own story. And not only that, we would also be able to describe our experiences as members of the group, and what the other dads had come to mean to us. And, most of all, we would be able to share our stories so that others might benefit from reading them.

A few of us had already written about our experiences with loss and grief, but most of us had not written anything. Some of us were not convinced we could even start. Some of us were not sure we wanted to write at all. Assistance was needed.

We were most fortunate to connect with Dianne Martin, a published author, an adjunct professor at Butler University, and an individual exuding grace, compassion, and understanding. After hearing about our group, meeting a few of us, and coming to a Tuesday morning breakfast, Dianne enthusiastically accepted the task of assisting us in writing our stories. She felt she was meant to do the project; she was correct. Without her personal encouragement and support, the book never would have been completed. To Dianne we offer our sincere and profound gratitude.

When the first draft of the manuscript was completed, it was shared with Tony Dungy, head coach of the Indianapolis Colts—2007 Super Bowl Champions. After reading it as a father who had also lost a son, he generously agreed to write the foreword. To Tony we offer our heartfelt appreciation for his warm support and his meaningful contribution.

From the beginning of the Dads Group there have been a number of other individuals who have been incredibly important to us. Foremost are our wives, or significant others, who have provided support and encouragement—day after day, year after year. Without them, and other family members, life would have been so much more painful and difficult to bear. To them we offer our steadfast love and enduring affection.

IN THE PAGES THAT FOLLOW YOU WILL FIND THE HEART WRENCHING STORIES OF 14 DADS AND HOW THEY FIND

MEANING AND HOPE THROUGH THEIR INTERACTION WITH EACH OTHER, BOTH IN WEEKLY BREAKFAST MEETINGS AND IN MANY OTHER ACTIVITIES THAT BRING TOGETHER TWO AND THREE—OR FOUR, FIVE AND SIX—OR AS MANY OF THE DADS WHO ARE INTERESTED—FOR SERIOUS DISCUSSIONS, MEMORIAL EVENTS, OR SOCIAL OCCASIONS AIMED AT JUST HAVING FUN.

THE DADS COME FROM ALL WALKS OF LIFE, INCLUDING A WIDE RANGE OF PROFESSIONS AND A BROAD SPECTRUM OF BELIEFS. THERE IS NO DOUBT, HOWEVER, THAT EACH DAD HAS RELIED ON SPIRITUAL FOUNDATIONS AND RESOURCES TO NAVIGATE THE DEPTHS OF GRIEF. AND EACH DAD WOULD ENCOURAGE YOU, WHATEVER YOUR BELIEFS, TO READ THESE STORIES WITH AN OPEN HEART AND MIND.

IT IS TO THIS END THAT THE BOOK IS WRITTEN: TO ENCOURAGE DADS WHO HAVE LOST A SON OR A DAUGHTER TO MEET—PERHAPS OVER A CUP OF COFFEE—AND TO SEE WHERE THE CONVERSATION MIGHT LEAD. IN ADDITION, IT IS WRITTEN TO ENCOURAGE OTHERS—MOMS, FAMILY MEMBERS, AND FRIENDS—WHO KNOW A DAD WHO HAS LOST A SON OR A DAUGHTER, TO SHARE THIS BOOK WITH HIM.

Foreword

THE NIGHT OF FEBRUARY 3ʀᴅ, 2007, I WAS IN A MIAMI HOTEL PRE-paring my team, the Indianapolis Colts, to face the Chicago Bears in Super Bowl XLI which would be played the following evening. On the eve of the biggest game in my coaching career, I had no way of knowing that something was taking place back in Indiana that would bring a new friend into my life.

In suburban Indianapolis Chuck and Becky Findley were preparing for the game as well. They were getting their home ready for the next day when they and their two boys, Jake and Travis, would watch their beloved Colts try to win a championship. It was going to be such a special day, with mom and dad sharing in what the boys loved to do—watch their Colts play.

I remember my last talk to the team that Saturday night. I told them that, although the whole country would be watching the Super Bowl and we wanted to do everything we could do to win and bring that trophy back to Indiana, that the Super Bowl was not the most important thing in the world. It was not life or death. I told them that being together on the journey and the joy of being a great "football family" were the things we would remember long after the game was over. I truly believed that, but it wasn't until after the game, when I would meet Chuck Findley, that I learned how true that really was.

You see, Jake and Travis Findley never got to see the game. That Saturday night the SUV they were riding in was hit by a train, killing both of them. I heard about the accident shortly after I got back to Indianapolis and it drained some of the joy out of that Super Bowl win for me. Reading the paper and seeing the headline of their accident just below our championship headline just didn't seem fair. At the time, I had no way of knowing that it would be the beginning of a special friendship with Chuck and, by extension, a kinship with thirteen other men.

I met Chuck in the spring of 2007 when I was contacted by Travis' teacher, who told me the third graders in his class were having trouble dealing with the fact that their friend was no longer there. Because I had lost a son the year before, she asked me if I would come and talk to the kids about how you deal with the death of someone very close to you. When I met the class we did talk some about death, but more of our time was spent talking about life—Travis' life, their life, and eternal life in heaven through Jesus Christ.

Tuesday Mornings with the Dads tells the stories of fourteen men who share the same thing in common—they've all lost children in one way or another. For anyone who has children, the stories will be gut-wrenching. But, just like my talk with the kids, the book is not as much about the loss of life as it is about living. It's about how these children lived, how they blessed their families and their communities. And, more than anything, it's about how their fathers have had to continue to live after their deaths. It tells about how these men have helped each other through the toughest thing a parent can go through.

These dads were brought together by tragedy and together they have worked their way through it. While none of them would say they're completely healed, they all feel that God has brought them together and allowed them to help each other. By writing this book, they will now help others—not only parents who've lost children but anybody who is facing unthinkable grief.

I know if you read this book you will take some great lessons with you. We can all learn something from these fourteen men. We will learn not to take the gift of children for granted. We'll learn that God is always present in our lives, even in the most difficult of circumstances. And most importantly, we'll learn that as important as it is to reach out to help others who are hurting, it's just as necessary to allow others to reach into our lives when we are experiencing pain. I'm very thankful that each of these men did that and I'm grateful to them for sharing their stories. I thank them for showing us that, no matter what the obstacles, with God's help—and with each other—we can persevere through anything life throws at us.

Tony Dungy

Our Group Begins

IT WAS TUESDAY MORNING, MAY 23, 2004. THE TIME WAS 7:00 a.m. A dad arrived and seated himself at a corner table in the coffee shop of an Indianapolis hotel. A second dad walked into the room, saw the person he was looking for, and sat down at the same table. A third dad entered, saw the other two, and pulled up a chair.

The three dads had met before, but didn't really know each other. Jerry Baker had lost his son, Jason, on September 17, 2001, just one week after 9/11. He had gone to a grief group composed of several women and one other man in March and April of 2003, but found he was not able to express himself in that group.

Mark Fritz had lost his son, Nick, on June 28, 2003. He had also attended a grief group of women and men in January and February of 2004, but was not comfortable in sharing what he was going through.

Adolf Hansen had lost his daughter, Bonnie, on May 11, 1996, the same day as his birthday and the eve of Mother's Day. He had been dealing with his grief in a variety of group settings over a period of several years, but had never met with just other dads.

All three of these dads had met before at St. Luke's United Methodist Church. Jerry had met Adolf on May 4, 2003, at the conclusion of a Sunday morning service where Adolf had spoken on the theme, "God Works for Good in Everything," and had included the story of the loss of his daughter. Mark had also met Adolf at church during the fall of 2003.

However, it was Marsha Hutchinson, a seminary student (now a pastor) working at St. Luke's, who had led a grief group to which Jerry had come, and another group to which Mark had come. Being aware that neither of them had shared deeply of themselves in those groups, Marsha let Jerry know there was another man she wanted him to meet. She said the same to Mark and then made arrangements to bring them together so they could tell their stories to each other.

After their initial sharing with each other, Marsha contacted Adolf, a colleague with whom she had worked for several months, and asked him if he would be interested in meeting with Jerry and Mark. His initial response was that he didn't want to become part of any group, but would join them one time.

The three dads met with Marsha the next Sunday afternoon at church. They shared their stories—briefly—and found they really could connect with each other. After nearly an hour had passed, Marsha asked if they wanted to meet again—without her. The dads weren't sure, but they concurred—not really knowing what that meant. Then one dad said to the other two, "Do you want to meet at church next Sunday afternoon?" The other two shook their heads. "I don't want to either. How about breakfast at 7:00 a.m. on the way to work?" Heads nodded. "Would the Omni Hotel at Shadeland and 82nd Street work for each of you?" Heads nodded again. The plan was to meet the following Tuesday morning. And this they did.

They met, exchanged words of greeting, ordered cups of coffee, and began talking and listening—learning more about each other as they tried to figure out what they were really doing, and why they were doing it. After some sharing had taken place, Adolf said, "I'm here as a dad, and nothing more." Mark was very quick to respond, "Whew! We don't need a chaplain!" Jerry readily agreed. And so they shared their stories in more detail—dad to dad to dad—nothing more.

The connection between these dads deepened that morning. The realization that kept surfacing for each of them was, "Wow! You guys really get it!" It was a remarkable time of sharing, so much so that the three dads decided to meet again the following Tuesday—yes, at 7:00 a.m., at the same table, in the same coffee shop. And this they did week after week after week.

It didn't take many weeks before these three dads shared who they were with Lori Carver, their server in the coffee shop. Her genuine smile and her caring presence made it easy to let her know they were dads who had lost a son or a daughter. And her empathetic response to this sharing encouraged further conversation. She didn't know much about these dads, but she seemed to understand what they were trying to do.

Sharing information about this group of three dads took place with others as well, especially with family members and close friends. And it wasn't long before the group broadened beyond members of St. Luke's. Two other dads joined the group in the summer of 2004. One was Steve Reed, who had lost his son, Greg, on June 8, 1999, though his body wasn't found until September 20 of that year. The other was Kim Manlove, who had lost his son, David, on June 9, 2001. At each of these times—and at all other times when another dad joined the group—the "old" dads retold their stories and then listened to the story of the "new" dad.

In the fall of that year, three additional dads came. Mike Laird had lost his son, Jake, on August 18, 2004—only a few months before joining the group. Jim Dodds had lost his daughter, Jenny, on June 16, 2001. Tom Harford had lost his son, Karl, on March 7, 2004.

Information about the dads group continued to spread by word of mouth. In the spring of 2005, two more dads came. Jerry Toomer had lost his son, Michael, on July 21, 1999. Anthony Pokorny had lost his daughter, Jennifer, on April 8, 2004. As a result there were now ten regular attendees on Tuesday mornings. It was uncommon for a dad to visit the group, and not continue coming. However, this did occur from time to time.

In the fall of 2005, three other dads came. Jon Pavey had lost his son, Jonathan, or "J. R." as he was known, on March 14, 2005. Rick Larrison had lost his son, Marc, on September 26, 2005—only eight days before coming to the group. Dave Toombs had lost his son, Adam, on April 9, 2005.

By this time two tables had been placed together to accommodate the group, even on Tuesdays when one, two, or three dads were absent due to work schedules, trips out of town, or other reasons for missing a meeting of the group. The possibility of sitting at two separate tables was discussed, but was quickly resisted. The dads wanted to be part of one group.

Seating became even more challenging as time went on. For, in the spring of 2006, three more dads showed up—each on a different Tuesday morning. Marv Hamilton, whose wife read about the group in a local paper and encouraged him to attend, had lost his son, Jeff, on July 24, 2005. Jim Barkley had lost his son, Colin, on March 1, 2006. Joe Leonard, who had to drive over an hour to get to the coffee shop, had lost his son, Charlie, on March 17, 2004.

On some Tuesday mornings a third table had to be added to the other two, particularly when virtually everyone was present. And this configuration continued with more regularity when two additional dads joined the group. Chuck

Findley, who had lost both of his sons, Jake and Travis, on February 3 and 4, respectively, 2007, came to the group in the spring of 2007—only a few weeks after their deaths. Chris O'Connor, who had lost his daughter, Keli, on July 10, 2005, joined the group in the summer of 2007.

Lori continued to be our server throughout this time. When dads were in deep conversation with each other, she would not interrupt to take orders for food—usually toast, bagel, muffin, cereal, fruit, or just coffee, or nothing at all. She would patiently wait, or leave and return a few minutes later. As a result she became a real friend to the dads. When she became pregnant with her second child, she endeared herself to the group even more. She was carrying a new life while the dads were grieving the loss of a life. On the Tuesday morning in August, 2005, when the dads gave her a gift card to celebrate the birth of her child, she was so surprised, and so touched, that tears welled up in her eyes, as they also did in the eyes of many fathers around the tables.

When Lori was offered a position in management with the company, she accepted and was no longer there on Tuesday mornings. She was truly missed, for she had become such an integral part of the group. In September of 2007, when it was her last day to work as a server, she was overwhelmed by the large amount of cash that was in the card she was given. She walked around the circle, hugged each dad, even the last two who had come—two whom she hardly knew. She wasn't going to leave anyone out.

Lori was—and is—a special person to the Dads Group! On one occasion she was heard saying, "I can tell there is a deep bond between you guys." She sensed this, in part, because she had observed the group; but she also sensed it because she had developed a bond with the dads. At each

Tuesday closest to Christmas she would leave a card on the table, with the envelope addressed to "my guys."

As the group evolved during these years, sharing deepened and broadened. Feelings of all sorts were disclosed, including tears as expressions of profound anguish and pain. Yes it was okay for men to show their emotions in this setting. It was a risk that could be taken because this was a safe place to really be yourself.

Yet—over time—other feelings surfaced as well. In the beginning there were few smiles and almost no laughter, but expressions of laughter began to interject themselves, and eventually the entire group could laugh together. One dad even said, "This is the only group where I can really laugh."

Sharing also broadened. At first, there was so much to explain regarding the tragedies each dad had experienced. And every time a new dad showed up, each dad told the story of his son's or daughter's death—usually in response to the new dad telling his story. As a result, the dads heard each other's story many times, and noticed that some of the stories became modified over time as candor increased and additional details came to light. Dads even helped each other clarify their stories as they made comments and asked questions.

Throughout this process—and even to the present day—there is no individual leader of the group. Yes, the three dads who met the first time did provide initial leadership, but the group evolved in such a way that leadership became collaborative. In other words, the group was never dependent on any one dad to lead.

The dads came to believe and practice their assumption that there were no rules in the group other than to show up. That was it—just show up! There were no other requirements, though there were some unspoken expectations that emerged: share only what you want to share; speak or be quiet, according to the mood you are in; give all who want to talk the opportunity to do so; be ready to listen with your heart as well as your head; know that you are cared for by the other dads in the group.

On some Tuesday mornings—though not all—one or another of the dads suggests that they go around the circle to get caught up with each other. And, again, over time, this sharing has broadened to include family matters, job related celebrations or concerns, as well as involvements in other settings such as scores in recent golf tournaments, or experiences on trips out of town. On other mornings the conversation may be a mixture of topics, from sports, to politics, to religion, to personal stories, even to jokes—some of which are great and others which are tolerated. There are also many email exchanges throughout the week covering these and other topics.

It is not uncommon for dads to greet each other on arrival. Likewise, when dads leave, either individually or as a group, they often hug each other, give and receive words of encouragement, or make plans to get together by twos, threes, or fours for other activities.

Hope keeps on surfacing in the group. The dads often provide it for each other—hope to make it through another day, hope to get through those difficult times (birth days, death days, and holidays), hope to find strength to go on, hope that more family members and friends will "get it," hope that meaning will be reconstructed, hope that good will come out of tragedy. And when one is lacking in hope, or wavering in hope, others in the group become sources of hope.

Trust also continues to emerge, as does sensitivity, compassion, and caring. Yet these qualities have taken time to develop—even in a group that is fairly homogeneous. The commonality that brought the group together was the recognition that each dad had lost a son or a daughter. Although the deaths were in many cases quite different—vehicular accident, misdiagnosis or negligence on the part of someone else, murder, drug addiction, the taking of one's own life— they were deaths that were sudden, unexpected, and tragic. There was little or no time to say goodbye. There was little or no time to grieve before the death occurred.

Each dad is encouraged by other dads in the group to grieve in his own way, in accordance with his own situation, his own personality, and his own grieving style. There is no judgment about right or wrong ways to do it. There is only encouragement to deal with it. Furthermore, there is no judgment of dads in relation to how the death took place. No dad is thought to be better than any other dad. And no dad is looked down upon—for any reason. Each dad lived in a way that showed deep caring for his son or daughter. The manner of death didn't change this at all.

The dads also learned to care about each other beyond the Tuesday morning gatherings. On January 25, 2005, a very cold and snow blowing morning, there was a dedication of the headstone for Mike Laird's son, Jake, at Crown Hill Cemetery. One dad in the group decided to attend. When he arrived he saw another dad was already there. Then a third dad showed up—and none of the dads knew the others were coming. A fourth dad came, but was so overcome with grief that he couldn't get out of his car.

On March 4, 2005, four of the dads drove to Muncie, Indiana, a town about fifty miles away, to be present in the courtroom with Tom Harford at the sentencing of the murderer of his son, Karl.

On June 26, 2005, five of the dads attended the dedication of a plaque in the courtyard of St. Luke's United Methodist Church in memory of Mark Fritz's son, Nick.

And on April 7, 2008, three of the dads drove to a rural location south of Greenwood, Indiana, a distance of nearly forty miles, to be present at the dedication of railroad crossing gates that had been installed at the location where the two sons of Chuck Findley, Jake and Travis, had been struck by a train and killed.

There were also many other times when dads demonstrated their care for each other. For example, when Joe Leonard became ill, had surgery, and unexpectedly ended up in the Cardiac Recovery Intensive Care Unit in St. Vincent Hospital, dads contacted him and his family, went to visit him, and were stunned when he suddenly died after only a short time following surgery. Many of the dads attended his visitation on October 19, 2007, and his funeral the next day. The card on the bouquet of flowers from the Dads Group read: "We love you like a brother."

Another example of caring was when Jim Barkley was suddenly and unexpectedly struck and critically injured by a car in downtown Indianapolis on May 7, 2008, a dark and rainy night, and taken to the Intensive Care Unit of Methodist Hospital. Several dads and their spouses visited with him and his wife on the day they received the news and several days thereafter, during his time of recuperation.

The relationship of spouses to the group began as soon as dads were at home and began to talk about their experiences on Tuesday mornings. And, as months passed by, interest grew in the possibility of including spouses in some type of social activity. The first was a dinner gathering in a private room at a nearby restaurant. It was an opportunity for spouses to meet each other as well as for dads to get to know other dads who, in some instances, were only names to them. Other social occasions followed in subsequent months in a variety of settings.

One of the places where some of the dads and their spouses connected was in church, particularly St. Luke's United Methodist Church, since a number of the dads are members there. However, there are other churches represented in the group as well—Presbyterian, Roman Catholic, and Baptist. In addition, there are dads who are not active in a local congregation.

The Dads Group has never been thought of as a church group, yet most of the dads have that connection. However, even for those who don't, there is an underlying faith in God that is very important to all the dads. It is one of the unifying forces that helps build cohesion in the group.

In addition to the incredible caring about each other, both on Tuesday mornings and at other times, there is the mutual support of the memorials that some of the dads have established. For example, three dads sponsor individual golf tournaments, two to raise funds for scholarships, and one to raise dollars for special needs in the police department. Another organizes a run and a walk through a scenic cemetery to raise dollars for a scholarship. Another sponsors a blood drive. Another sponsors teams of runners and walkers to raise funds for the American Heart Association. Another raises funds to build arms at railroad crossings. Still others have established endowed college scholarships, recognizing students in a way that pertains to the son or daughter being honored, whether relative to one's major field of study, or one's activity in a project such as a mission trip to another part of the world.

Those in this dads group believe that good can come out of tragedy. And that is the primary reason for writing this book: to tell the stories of their sons and daughters and, as a part of those narrations, to share how the Dads Group has helped them work through their grief and reconstruct their meaning—in healthy, creative, and productive ways—in a world that has been radically changed.

Adolf Hansen

OUR STORIES

Jason Matthew Baker

SEPTEMBER 25, 1976 – SEPTEMBER 17, 2001

THE SUMMER OF 2000, MY OLDEST SON JASON AND I HAD JUST finished hiking the Grand Canyon. We had trekked to Phantom Ranch at the bottom of the Canyon and back in one day. Not a major accomplishment in this day and age of extreme outdoor enthusiasts, but a dream fulfilled for someone over fifty. Over 50, Wow! Did I ever think my parents were old at this age? But here I was with my son, who was probably pretty impressed the "old man" could do this in the summer heat of July.

But that is how we were that day. My adult son, twenty-two at the time, had blisters on his feet just like I did, but refused to do anything but admire the beautiful vista, having met the challenge, and appreciate our time together.

In January, 2002, I hiked that trail again. This time alone, and this time to scatter some of Jason's ashes along the path we had traveled less than two years before.

I stood on the rim of that canyon and thought about how free it would be to float on the wind like Jason's ashes. To be free from these earthly bonds that have hung on me like a wet wool blanket for the past months since his death. It wasn't suicide that was in my mind and heart, it was just the need to not hurt anymore. I did not want to kill myself; I think I just didn't care if I lived anymore. If I could just be with him again … even for a few minutes. I think this is a pretty normal feeling; after a loss, it's all about no time for goodbyes. That prevailing thought was the culmination of months of grieving following my son's death.

This is how my life changed in an instant.

I am a police officer and had been, at the time of Jason's death, for over thirty years. Life was in order. I was content. My children were doing well, I loved what I did, and I was involved in the community in a variety of ways, especially coaching soccer, baseball and basketball with my kids' teams. My wife worked in the not-for-profit sector. Serving our community was something we had both done our entire lives. Our passion to serve helped to instill in our kids something about giving back to the community and developing a strong work ethic.

Jason was the oldest. From about the time he was five years old, he wanted to be a police officer. I was Chief of Police in a small Michigan town, and Jason would come to the police station after school to work on his homework and talk with members of the department. Around town he was known to most as Chief Baker's boy. Many times I would tell him that he had plenty of time for law enforcement after college. I even suggested that he might find something else he liked to do that would not include working weekends and holidays, and that maybe even paid a little more. Yet he was determined.

As he grew older Jason joined the police explorers. At thirteen years old, proudly wanting to follow in his father's footsteps, he was not afraid to join a group that wasn't the most popular for a junior high school student. He persevered and followed the explorers with the police cadet program designed for high school age kids. Jason also excelled in community service and his studies. He received an award for the total number of community service hours he had achieved, that still stands to this day. Academically, he was named as an honor graduate. Upon graduation, it was off to college— something his mother and I had expressed as fact from his earliest beginnings.

After his freshman year, Jason returned home and began working for the local sheriff's department as a civilian dispatcher. He soon became very proficient and made a name for himself. Jason was the communications specialist of choice anytime he was working and there was a tactical call out, because he was that good. As the summer drew to a close, he asked if he could keep working and transfer his college credits from Indiana University in Bloomington, to Indiana University Purdue University in Indianapolis, where we now lived. He promised he would finish his degree as he worked full-time. This would allow him to continue to work towards his goal of law enforcement while getting his education.

He kept his promise while achieving his law enforcement dream. It wasn't long before he was assigned to the road as a jail wagon driver. He soon ingratiated himself to the full-time deputies working the street. Our next surprise came when he got a job as a full-time road deputy. The problem was, he needed to attend a fifteen-week state certified academy in order to meet the state's guideline for full-time officers. This meant he would have to miss a semester of school. Again, he promised he would continue his education as soon as he was out of training, and he would finish his degree. He always kept his word, so we gave our blessing. As a father, I felt great pride that my son would want to follow in my career path.

So it was off to the training academy. At the end of the training there is a formal graduation ceremony. Jason did not know it, but the state director of the training academy had asked me to deliver the graduation address. We kept that secret from him until the day before graduation, when the official programs were delivered. It was a very proud moment for my son and me, to be together, in uniform. Jason began his career and, true to his word, re-enrolled in college.

In 2001, Jason was getting close to his third-year anniversary on the job. The attacks of September 11 put everyone in law enforcement on high alert. When we weren't working, or Jason was not in school, we would talk about what a life-changing event this was going to be for America. But that was then.

On Sunday, September 16, Jason was over for a cookout; played with his brother and sister; and he and I enjoyed some time alone on the back deck. The next day, September 17, 2001, we both worked. We were on different departments but working the same county. He worked 3-11 p.m. and I worked 4-midnight.

Often we would communicate electronically over the computers in the police car. It was an eerily quiet Monday, without many runs for anybody. Our only contact that evening had been a computer message about a "slow night."

Then, a little after 7 p.m., I heard a home invasion alarm go out and my son answered that he would respond. Less than sixty seconds into the run, he was disregarded, and a closer police officer took that call.

About fifteen minutes later, a multi-agency emergency broadcast came out declaring a Code 1. That means a law enforcement officer is declaring a life-threatening emergency. In this case the broadcast was that, "County 232 is taking fire." 232 was Jason's radio number. As I heard bits and pieces of radio traffic, I learned that my son was chasing a car, and the occupants were firing what would turn out to be an AK-47 assault rifle at him. My "child" was in danger so I started for the area. I heard portions of my son's transmissions on the radio. I had to drive carefully because every officer within a few miles was doing the same thing I was. We were all desperately trying to reach Jason. I heard my son on the radio ... then all I heard were other officers.

I was working my way to the area of the chase when I called my wife and told her that Jason was involved in something serious. I told her I thought he had been shot. As I reflected back on this moment, and after listening to the entire tape of the event, I discovered that the call had not gone out yet confirming he had been shot. Because I no longer heard my son on the radio, I somehow knew; I felt the parental instinct that said something was wrong. I told my wife to get someone to the house to be with her and I would call her back.

Someone finally was able to get through on the radio that an officer had been shot. Another officer, Jerry Durham, a friend and shift mate of my son's, screamed for everybody to hold their radio traffic, and directed dispatch to contact 232. He had the same premonition that I had had; not hearing Jason on the radio could only mean one thing. Then the sole voice of the dispatcher calling 232 was met with no answer, only silence. I got to the scene, which was chaotic. The suspects had fled on foot and shots were still being fired and exchanged with police. As I arrived to the last known location of my son and got out of my car, a deputy looked at me, shook his head, and said Jason had just left in the ambulance. Needing to get to my son, I headed to the hospital.

I don't remember where I parked—I just pulled into the emergency room area. The ambulance was empty and the doors opened automatically before me. This moment is like slow motion. Every person was looking at me, yet no one spoke. Some just pointed down a hall and I turned toward the trauma units. I was met at the door to a room, and someone tried to keep me out, but without speaking I just went in. No one was working on Jason. The rational part of my brain told me what I had already suspected. The emotional side paralyzed me. He was warm; his head wound was leaking blood. If blood is coming out, the heart must be beating? I heard someone say he never made it to the hospital.

The next several hours are a blur. Police officers, chaplains, and dignitaries all came to the hospital. At one point I went out to catch a breath of fresh air, to find what must have been two hundred police officers outside the hospital. They were all just standing there. This was remarkable, because the suspects who had caused this were still not in custody.

Next, my life became a blur.

Get up, do something, and try not to fall apart too much. I was a police officer and a man; we kept things to ourselves and protected our families. I was doing the best I could for my family, but I was really just going through the motions. I was stuck.

Several months after Jason's death, I overheard one of my daughter Gabrielle's friends ask if there was anything she could do for her. There was a pause, and then Gabrielle said, "I want my dad back." I realized then, that I was physically there, but emotionally somewhere else. I was lost and not much good to anyone.

I had support at work from my good friend Diane, who understood grief. She gave me space, but was a safety net. But even her help wasn't enough. There was a hole in my heart that could never be fixed. This experience had changed my life forever, unlike anything I had ever experienced before. This included over thirty years in law enforcement and a tour of duty in Vietnam. But worse, I couldn't figure out how to let life in again. And that is what brought me back to the rim of the Canyon on a cold January day.

I had no plan other than to hike down as far as I felt like hiking, and to scatter Jason's ashes somewhere along the trail, at one of the many points where he and I had stopped to take pictures the summer a year before. Because of the snow and cold, I was alone on the trail, and perhaps that was a good thing. Like I had done on the drive out to the Canyon, I cried uncontrollably at times. For the first time in my life, there was no light at the end of the tunnel. As I hiked, many thoughts and images came and went. But then, it hit me, WWJD? What would Jason do! Always optimistic, he would say, "Dad, this is the greatest job in the world. How many people get paid to do what they love to do—and if I had to die, I did it doing my job." I don't know where it was exactly, but sometime after scattering some of Jason's ashes, and planting a small American flag on which I had written a personal message, I headed back home, hoping to be a better person. Easier said than done.

I got involved in some grief crisis counseling of my own. I went to some training, learned a lot of things about myself under the guise of helping others. This training allowed me to meet a friend who has helped me more than any counseling.

Just a few years after Jason's death, our city suffered another terrible death of a police officer. This officer, too, had been killed by an automatic assault rifle. I was asked to go to the hospital to meet the family. It was the same hospital my son had been in. I was told the family was on their way in and would I take them to see their son. I asked to see their son first, so that I could better control my emotions with the parents. I was taken to the same room where my son had been. On the table this time was another young officer, Jake Laird, without the signs of significant trauma; and, like my son, he had not survived the ride to the hospital.

I was told the parents were arriving. I stood in front of the automatic emergency room doors. As before, when the doors opened there was silence from everyone, but this time I was there to escort them on one of the longest walks of life a parent has to take. That is how I met Mike and Debbie Laird, Jake's father and mother. I wanted to be there for Mike, because I knew what was ahead for him. Mike and I, to this day, are very best friends. Mike is on my speed dial, because he gives as much as he gets. He sometimes calls and asks how I am doing, which is code for he is having a bad moment, and then it is okay after we talk. I do the same with him.

Before I met the Lairds, I went to church, didn't go to church, talked to a psychologist, talked to a crisis interventionist ... and still I wasn't who I was before. I wasn't taking care of business the way I should with my family. I was angry and short most of the time, because I saw my family disintegrating around me and I could not fix it. I was a very closed-off person; the pain did not hurt as much if I guarded against talking about it. I started attending a couples grief counseling session (not my first attempt at group therapy). It was mostly women, and I was there in body only. Yes, men and women do grieve differently. The facilitator Marsha Hutchinson, both a minister and a counselor, took me aside after a few sessions and stated, sort of like a question, that I wasn't getting much out of this? Being brutally honest is one of my new traits and I said she was correct. She told me she had another father who could benefit from talking to me (tricky Marsha, making me think I was doing this other dad a favor). I agreed to meet him and she set a meeting up for a Sunday afternoon at church.

I credit Marsha Hutchinson for having the unselfish insight to recognize that the best help she could offer to me while in her counseling group, was to put me in touch with someone else in the same situation. How wonderful to have a person who truly cared about helping someone in her group—by directing them in another direction. That single act of compassion was the start of a light at the end of my dark tunnel.

I went into that meeting with no expectations. Nothing had been working, so I would give meeting with another dad a try. I could at least tell everyone I was trying to do something. It was there that I met Mark Fritz, a dad about my age who had lost his son. In less than fifteen minutes Mark and I agreed to meet again, because we both had sensed something in the other. We agreed to meet in a morning session, not afternoon, and to meet at a restaurant (neutral place) and not a church. We set up the meeting for the next Tuesday (men act—we need to *do* something). Mark and I met on a Tuesday morning and passed nearly ninety minutes without any thought for how much time we were spending together. I am sure we both came to that first meeting with built-in excuses about a pending meeting, in case this encounter did not work out. But that wasn't the case with either of us. The conversation was easy, our pent-up feelings were mutual. Like anger, guilt, the feeling of failing my family, and not caring about not caring! It wasn't sympathy I was seeking; in fact I avoided people and situations where that might happen. All the other feelings that I thought made me crazy, Mark was having too. I was normal, dealing with an abnormal situation.

The next meeting was even more in depth. Mark's son had died of a drug overdose, my son died a hero's death, yet Mark and I were both the same. I don't want to speak for Mark, but for me, having someone who truly understood how I felt—the anger, the guilt, the remorse, and the loss of love of life, to name just a few feelings—was like a life preserver. We could talk about the roller coaster of emotions and feelings that we both felt, feelings we would never share with an outsider—someone who had not been through this. I was a different person, and so was Mark, after that meeting. Maybe I was going to make it after all.

Our third meeting included another man from the same church who was a co-worker of Marsha's—Adolf Hansen. I invited my new friend, Mike Laird, to the meetings, and then he invited a friend, and then there were five … six … and then sixteen. All the circumstances of death were different, but every man's story, to me, was as bad and devastating as mine. If they can do it, so can I.

I miss very few Tuesday mornings. I think my wife would not let me, even if I tried. Yes the difference is noticeable. The group does not change the circumstances of my grief; the group just lets me know that my feelings are my own and that it is okay to feel the way I feel. The fact of missing my son is going to be with me for the rest of my life, but I can manage it. I will never get over it, but I am getting past it. I am there for the other dads, and they are there for me. Sometimes the talk is serious and sometimes it is light. I sometimes miss the intimacy of the smaller group, but being a part of a larger special group is comforting and safe.

I haven't told the whole story of my son's death, because this is about living after such an event. This is about feeling a certain way when everyone around you feels differently because they don't understand. I hated the holidays, still do, but like the other dads, it's okay. My family takes two cars to gatherings and I leave after awhile, because it is hard to be there when a loved one is missing; but everyone understands, and most importantly I can do this without guilt, because it is a normal feeling.

I've returned to the Canyon for a third visit, and to scatter more of Jason's ashes, and I can't help but stand on the rim and smile. This time, at the wonderful memories my son and I had here, and all the other times we had together. Does it still hurt as much? Absolutely! Do I still have feelings of guilt? Yes I do. Am I angry? Yes I am. Sometimes at God, sometimes at all the people who go through life and do not appreciate the moments they have. I still cry at times. I never finish a conversation with my children without saying, "I love you." I also am not afraid to tell another man in our group that I love him, too. Am I the same dad and husband I once was, before my son was killed? No, my life is forever changed—but now I have a lifeline that is only a Tuesday morning or a phone call away. I can, and have, picked up the phone ... or just dropped in on my friend Mike or another "dad" ... and it's like being in a very safe place. It's that hug that men don't do.

Jason grew up in the shadow of my career. He was known as Chief Baker's son around town. Now, in the law enforcement community, I am known as Jason Baker's father. I hope I can live up to that title with the same dignity, grace, and honor that Jason did.

"I love you and miss you,"
Dad

Jerry Baker

Ralph Nicholas "Nick" Fritz

JANUARY 5, 1980 – JUNE 28, 2003

I THINK I WILL START MY STORY OF NICK WHERE WE START THE group. His story.

Nick died at age twenty-three, after ten years of struggling with drugs. He began using drugs walking home from school in the eighth grade, when a friend offered him LSD, and I suspect he never was truly clean again until his death. Nick, his family and friends struggled through arrest and time in jail at least three different events. He participated in three and maybe more rehabilitation programs. He went to a private lockdown school, and there was introduced to hard drugs like heroin and cocaine. His ability to find drugs, alcohol, and pills was unending. The disease of drug addiction overwhelmed him and our family for those terrible ten years.

Nick without the disease was a great kid, liked and loved by everyone. He had the warm engaging personality that pulled people to him. People liked just being around him. While he struggled with grades, he was the center of social life in school. He also received, from his mother's side, wonderful athleticism and was a beautiful roller blader, ice skater, and water skier. He knew X sports before they had a name. Some favorite pictures of Nick have him jumping cars roller blading, skating the hockey ice, and sailing through the sky water skiing. His grace was palpable.

Nick left a wife, Lindsay, and son, Kuai. His daughter Kaiya was born four months after his death. His children look just like him, and his son has his same reserved comfortable personality. He left a mother, stepfather, stepmother, me, three brothers, four sisters, brother-in-law, sister-in-law, and a nephew and niece. So much family and yet such a deep hole.

The gene for addiction came from my side of the family. Alcohol abuse is widespread in my family. I am sorry to have handed him this burden. Because of the addiction, Nick and I did not talk the last year of his life. I thought he would get clean and we would reconcile some day. I suspect we will still reconcile some day, just not the way I had hoped.

Lindsay

Lindsay was a half sister to Nick, and ten years younger. He was a hero to her. Nick was always playful and full of fun and games when he was around his brothers and sisters. Within three months of his death, Lindsay started cutting on herself and had suicide notes and plans shortly thereafter. Learning from Nick, we moved quickly to get her in counseling and inpatient programs. While the suicide issue passed, Lindsay's desire to follow Nick's path was unwavering. A gift to us from Nick was "tough love" and we moved to include law enforcement quickly in Lindsay's treatment plan. After a three-year hell with Lindsay, including her being removed from our homes and placed in a residential high school, she has emerged with a passion for life and a clean lifestyle.

After this was first written, Lindsay had a major relapse, but she is again clean and trying to put her life back together. She is living with her mother, working, and preparing to return to school, training to be a medical assistant. The impact of her relapse took a major toll on the entire family as we relived her and Nick's drug addiction issues. This disease never ends.

I share the story of Lindsay, and the positive outcome, because no one prepares the grieving parents for the issue of losing other children, yet our group has seen significant issues with siblings of the lost child. There is no time to grieve when you are scrambling to not lose a second child.

Blessings

Periodically, something will happen and I will explain it as another gift from Nick. He keeps giving gifts to us.

His children Kuai and Kaiya, their mother (also named Lindsay), Robert (her new husband), and James (Robert's son)—Nick's reconstituted family—have proven to be a blessing as they have continued forward with a drug-free lifestyle and love for their children. The gift of grandchildren is a true major blessing from Nick.

This group of men, the fathers group, has proven to be a base of love and friendship I would have never known without this event. One father says we paid too large a price to join this club, but this is where we find ourselves. So much solace and kindness has come from this group. The understanding and hugs of other men has meant much to me. No one understands the pain of losing a child like someone who has been there.

My understanding of God has increased dramatically since Nick died. I believe God answered my prayer. I had asked God to heal Nick or take him to his side, because his disease was overwhelming for all of us here on earth. While I did not agree with God's decision to take him to his side, I have come to realize that he is the ultimate authority and does know best. My prayer life and commitment to my faith have increased dramatically as well. I find that those in the fathers group are men of faith who have also had significant changes in their faith life after their experience.

An increased comfort with my own mortality has grown from Nick's loss. I find that I am ready if God decides now is my time. I have seen so much of life, and have come to know its ultimate ups and downs to such an extent, that I am appreciative of the experience and am ready should God call me home.

In making funeral and burial arrangements for Nick, cremation had not been an alternative for me until I learned that Nick had talked about and wanted this. With his cremation, and the grace of his services, I have come to a new comfort level with this for myself. I am now able to articulate my plans and prepare to help my family with these difficult issues for myself.

Time reallocation has changed dramatically for me, too. I don't care about many of the activities and issues I cared about before Nick died. Money and its pursuit has become a non issue for me. I just don't care about what I have or live with any more. Simplicity and balance have come into my life for the first time. This has created issues for me, because I do not make sense to those who have known me best. I have changed from the inside out on this issue. Time alone with my children, grandchildren, family and friends has become my new priority. Frankly, those around me do not quite know how to handle this. I've lost a marriage due to these changes.

Priority-setting follows the above paragraph. I think about activities, and where they fall in my priorities, and take action based on that. Again, this is not understood by those closest to me, who have come through the years with me. I have lost friends, and friendships have changed due to this.

The University family that surrounded me dumbfounded me. I was a staff person with the University of Indianapolis, and I was astounded by how that family wrapped itself around me to care for me. The attention and acts of kindness were unbelievable and I have never been able to thank them enough.

The friends who rallied around us at Nick's death, also were unbelievable. Kit, my college roommate, who made his home our home for the week of the funeral. Rick, my attorney, who called every morning for six months after Nick's death, to be sure I was doing okay. The friend of my wife who came to the house and boated with us the afternoon we heard about Nick, doing nothing more than being with us. Sharon, the friend of my wife who brought the ham to our house that we ate all week. Simple acts of caring and kindness that were unexpected but appreciated so much.

Little blessings along the way have continued and seem to be unending. Acts of kindness from friends and strangers take on new meaning now. Little remembrances go so far!

And yet, I would give up every blessing for one more day with Nick.

The Fathers Group

My grief has taken some strange paths in the five-plus years since Nick's death. At first, like many men, I plunged myself into work and ignored the inner signals. After a year, my wife and I did some group work at church, but I found that scratched the surface. Then, Marsha brought Jerry Baker and me together. The bond and outpouring was immediate. My son the drug addict and his son the hero left the same thing behind—fathers with big holes in their chests. Gaping holes that bled, and hurt, and were unfillable. Adolf joined us and we knew the feelings were not just ours.

Each father—those that have come and stayed, and those that have come and gone—has felt the thing no one can explain. We each "get it" and know immediately the hurt and pain that is so different from our wives' or children's pain. As real, but different. I never miss this group if I am in town. These are men I would never have known—"the group no one wishes to join"—and my connection is as real and deep as any male connection of my life. Each is friend, brother, lover in a new way for me. Only through our talks have I found growth and hope in my son's death.

Future

I hope for the day when I can again feel unlimited joy. I suspect I may never. Every emotion, every event of my life, has a limiter and governor in place. A fear pervades my days and creates space that something will happen to another child of mine. Such a piece of me went to the grave with Nick. I fear I will reclaim that piece only at my own death, my chance to see Nick again. I long to see Nick again, ask for him to appear in my dreams. I believe he is around, particularly when I am with his children.

Until then, I meet with my fellow fathers, work, play, love and miss. Of all the roles in life I play, I am a father first. Nick helped me to know this.

Mark Fritz

Bonnie Hansen Bromund

JULY 3, 1964 – MAY 11, 1996

IT WAS A FRIDAY EVENING. THE DATE WAS MAY 10, 1996. I HAD just arrived home. Tears were already rolling down my cheeks as I opened the door. There stood my wife, Naomi, looking as distraught as I've ever seen her. We embraced immediately and sobbed in each other's arms.

I didn't want to let go, but I became aware of other people in the room. First I saw my pastor, Phil. We hugged as we cried. Then I saw my assistant from work, Sally, who is also Phil's wife. We also hugged as we cried. Then the doorbell rang and there stood my supervisor from work, Neal, the president of the seminary. We also embraced with tears flowing freely.

I don't remember any words that were spoken, except for those that Naomi and I shared as we recounted what we had heard. There had been a series of phone calls. The first one had come to Naomi at home in Evanston, Illinois. The message was that our daughter Bonnie, who lived in Indianapolis, Indiana, had been hit by a vehicle and had been taken to the hospital. Details were unknown.

The message was immediately relayed to me in my office. It was after 4:30 p.m. The office was officially closed. I was reviewing words of tribute that I had written for a faculty colleague who was soon to retire and was being honored that evening. As I hung up the phone I went straight to the president's office to let him know that he might need to pinch-hit for me. I gave him a copy of what I had prepared.

As he was reviewing the text, his phone rang. He indicated Naomi was on the line and handed the receiver to me. I listened very intently as I heard her tell me she had just received another call from a family member in Indianapolis. "They've done all they can," she said, "but there doesn't seem to be any hope." I asked questions. Naomi answered as best she could, but she had been given very few details. Then she added, "I think they said they're going to try to keep her alive until tomorrow." My heart sank. I stopped breathing momentarily, and then burst into tears like a volcano suddenly erupting. I'll never forget that moment. "Then she's really died," I said to Naomi. "Uh huh," I heard in response.

I hurriedly left my tribute with Neal and asked him to present it on my behalf, but not to indicate what had happened. I didn't want to spoil the evening for three of my faculty colleagues who were being recognized for their illustrious careers.

It was the details that we had heard in those phone calls that Naomi and I were now sharing with Phil, Sally, and Neal. It became clear to all of us—rather quickly—that Naomi and I needed to leave right away for Indianapolis, a trip of 210 miles.

The five of us decided to join together in prayer. We stood, formed a circle and held hands. And, as we were doing this, some words came out of my mouth without any forethought at all. I heard myself saying, "Whatever happens, we're going to trust God."

I don't remember any other words that were spoken in that circle. Phil, Sally, and Neal probably said some very thoughtful things. They always do. Each of them probably prayed a very thoughtful prayer, but all I remember is that they were there. They had come right away. They had shown that they cared. They had joined with us in our excruciating pain.

I kept saying the words to myself over and over again, "Whatever happens, we're going to trust God." They were words springing up from the core of my being. They were comforting. They were strengthening. They were energizing. They served like an anchor to a boat caught in a raging storm.

Trust in the Lord with all your heart, and do not rely on your own insight.

Proverbs 3:5

The ride from Evanston to Indianapolis was very difficult, both intellectually and emotionally. The Friday evening traffic through Chicago was incredible. The usual trip of less than four hours took over five hours that night. As we slowly made our way through Chicago, we made calls to the hospital from our car. We began to put some pieces together. Bonnie had been struck by a city bus as she was crossing the street in downtown Indianapolis on her way home from work. She had lost consciousness immediately upon impact, had been taken to the hospital, had undergone surgery to explore the extent of injury to her head, had been diagnosed as unable to survive, and was being kept alive by numerous procedures, devices, and medications until we could get there, and until arrangements could be made for her organs to be donated and transplanted.

Bonnie was a highly respected and greatly loved daughter. She had been an excellent student with nearly a straight-A record through high school, had been an Honor Scholar all four years at DePauw University, had gone to law school at Indiana University, and had passed the bar exam in Indiana a semester before graduation.

Bonnie was also a faithful and vibrant follower of Jesus Christ, and believed her faith and her intellectual pursuits were complementary, and needed to be integrated with each other. She also believed that responding to the needs of others was essential to living out her faith. Therefore, she worked very closely with the University Chaplain at DePauw and, in her senior year, became the coordinator of all the January Winter Term in Mission trips. She herself went to Costa Rica one year and Sierra Leone another year.

Remembering who Bonnie was, and all the promise she embodied, made the trip to Indianapolis so indescribably painful. And what intensified the pain even further, was the realization that she would likely be pronounced dead the next day, May 11th, my birthday. I sobbed so heavily as I realized this, that I couldn't utter a word. At times it was very difficult to see the road through my tears. And, as if this were not enough, Naomi realized that Bonnie's death would come on Saturday, the eve of Mother's Day.

The details of the next twenty-four hours would take too long to describe in a summary such as this. So much happened. So many people were involved. So much anguish was felt.

After staying up all night and the entire next day, we concurred with the medical staff and joined them in pronouncing Bonnie dead at 6:15 p.m. Family members and a variety of caregivers joined Naomi and me as we held hands in a large circle around the bed—a circle that included the hands of Bonnie. We committed her life to God, and prayed for the medical teams that would remove her organs and transplant them into others who were unknown to us.

Throughout those very, very difficult hours I found myself still trusting God in the midst of my pain. I hurt so deeply, yet I trusted God as deeply as I hurt. And, though I didn't expect it, my experience of intertwining the two became indescribably profound. Nothing was going to destroy my trust in God, not even the death of my beloved daughter!

Waking up in a strange hotel room on Mother's Day, Naomi and I could scarcely believe we would never see Bonnie alive again. The day before seemed like a dream, yes, a nightmare. Yet we knew Bonnie was dead. Even though it was hard to believe, it was true. Even though it didn't seem real, it was.

So much more happened on that Sunday as calls/flowers/visitors arrived, on that Monday when funeral arrangements had to be made, on that Tuesday when hundreds of people came to the visitation to share in our grief, on that Wednesday when several hundred more came to attend the funeral service at Meridian Street United Methodist Church and to see her casket—now closed—at the front of the altar rail, the very location where she had been married ten months earlier.

Much more continued to happen in the weeks and months that followed. Yet, through it all, I didn't find myself feeling anger toward God for what had happened. I was certainly angry with the bus driver for turning into a pedestrian walkway without paying attention, and for hitting Bonnie very forcefully as she crossed with the right of way on a green light, but I eventually worked through those feelings.

As the summer went on I found myself wondering if I was denying my anger toward God. I thought about it over and over again, very intentionally and very honestly. Was my repetition of the phrase, "Whatever happens, we're going to trust God," a way of not dealing with the harshness of what had happened? I thought about it very diligently.

At the same time, I knew I'd faced harshness all of my life—directly, candidly, and in full view. I had learned that, for me, it made more sense to deal with reality just the way it was. Perhaps that's why, before Naomi and I returned to our home in Evanston, we went to the accident scene and stood at the edge of the street. With tears streaming down our faces, we watched as buses entered the pedestrian walkway precisely where Bonnie was killed. We wanted to face the stark reality of what had happened.

As the summer drew to a close, I began to realize— through my reflecting and praying—that something else had happened in my life years before. It was twenty years earlier, in 1976, that my other beloved daughter Becky, at age 14, had been diagnosed with diplopia (double vision) and pap-illedema (a swelling of the optic nerve caused by a rise in pressure within the brain). That startling news also came on a Friday afternoon. And, by the following Monday, she was in the hospital for tests. Then, about a week later, she began a series of nine major surgeries. The first one tried to remove a growth that was blocking the fluid from moving through the ventricular system of her brain, but couldn't. A shunt was surgically placed to bypass the blockage. Eight more surgeries followed in the next three years, including the removal of a substantial section of her skull to stop the bleeding from a massive subdural hemorrhage on the right side of her head. The threat of death came repeatedly. At one of those times, the doctors indicated they had done all they could and that we should be aware that she might very well die. It was so serious that we even began making funeral arrangements.

It was during those three years that I became aware of my anger toward God, admitted it, allowed it to surface in some very torturous ways, and worked through it. I did this—over time—as I kept on processing my feelings and reconstructing my meaning. Therefore, I didn't have much ongoing anger after Bonnie's death. I did have incredible pain and anguish, day after day, week after week, month after month. However, in the midst of this intense struggle, I was privileged to have many resources to help me deal with it.

First of all, there was my very dear wife, Naomi. We had been married for 37 years at the time Bonnie died. And during those years we had developed a very deep sense of respect, love, and trust in each other.

Second, there was our older daughter, Becky, who had come through three years of very serious medical circumstances, and had recovered far beyond our expectations, and far beyond the expectations of her doctors. She was such an encouragement to us as was her son, Michael, who had been born a year before Bonnie died.

Third, there were so many friends who responded to us, not only at the time of Bonnie's death, but consistently thereafter—for years to come—even to the present day. And with many of these friends we had, and still have, deep trust relationships.

Fourth, there were also those with whom we worked— some of whom were also close friends. Naomi's colleagues— teachers, administrators, parents—were very thoughtful and supportive. My colleagues at the theological seminary where I taught and served as a vice president—faculty, administrators, staff, students, and members of the board of trustees—were very sensitive, empathetic, and resourceful. I had never been cared for by such a large number of individuals in such powerful ways. I had never been hugged by so many people so many times.

The reception I received when I returned to work about a week after Bonnie's funeral was so meaningful—day after day after day—that it allowed me to be very open about what had happened, and about what was happening in my ongoing experience of it. I told my story over and over again, sharing my feelings as well as my thoughts, my tears as well as my words, not dozens of times, but hundreds of times. And my colleagues listened with such earnestness and such tenderness—men as well as women.

In the midst of all of these relationships, there was one other resource that was at the depth of my being, namely, my trust relationship with God. Knowing that God was good, and that God worked for good in everything, were beliefs that enabled me to experience God as an ally, not an enemy. Knowing that God's steadfast love was with me, and would continue to stay with me, regardless of what might happen, was a profound source of strength—and still is today. And because Naomi, Becky, and so many of my friends and colleagues also had a very similar trust relationship with God, I felt a deep bond with them, one that was very powerful. It was expressed in a variety of ways, but none as powerful as when they prayed, not only for me, but with me.

Seven years of grieving had taken place before I came to Indianapolis and met Jerry Baker on Sunday morning, May 4, 2003. Another six months took place before I met Mark

Fritz. And by the time I met with Jerry and Mark in the coffee shop on May 23, 2004, it had been eight years since Bonnie had died.

In addition to the lapse of time since Bonnie's death, there was also my ongoing work in research, writing, and teaching on the subject of death and dying. Prior to May 11, 1996, I had taught a course. "The Meaning of Death," five times at the University of Indianapolis. I had also taught a course, "Death, Grief, and Bereavement," two times at Indiana University School of Medicine. In addition, I had led numerous continuing education events during those years.

After a couple of years had passed since Bonnie's death, my colleagues at the seminary began encouraging me to consider writing and/or teaching in the field of death and dying once again, and to incorporate my own experience of losing a daughter. With their support and their input, I developed a course, "Loss and Grief," and began teaching it in 2001, and every other year since then—up to the present day. Revisiting attachment theory in more detail, I wrote a book, *Responding to Loss: A Resource for Caregivers,* published by Baywood in 2004.

With this opportunity to incorporate Bonnie's death into my academic experience, and having had a time period of eight years to carry on this process, I was not drawn to meeting with two dads on an ongoing basis. I agreed to meet them at church and then, after sharing an initial version of our story, to have a follow-up conversation to finish this sharing.

However, after I spent some time with Jerry and Mark, two very thoughtful and compassionate dads, I began to change my mind. They really understood what I had experienced in losing Bonnie. They really got it! And they got it at a much deeper level than most people I had told my story to earlier. I also got it when they told their stories. It was a connection between dads that was really special.

I had never had the experience of meeting with other dads who had lost a son or a daughter and sharing so openly and forthrightly with each other. Yet I wondered in those weeks of early summer in 2004 how long we would keep on meeting. We hadn't planned on organizing a group. But a fourth dad showed up after hearing about our breakfast meeting on Tuesday mornings. Our conversation broadened to include his experience. Then a fifth dad came and our conversation broadened even further. And I found myself not only wanting to go, but hoping the meetings would continue. I was "hooked" and was finding it very meaningful to be "a dad, and nothing more."

My participation in the Dads Group from the beginning allowed me to get acquainted with each dad as he joined the group. I realized months later how much more difficult it was for a dad to meet six, eight, or ten dads the first time he came to the group, and not get confused as to who was who, and what circumstances belonged to which dad.

As I listened to the story each dad told when he came to the group, I realized there were both similarities and differences. What we had in common provided points of connection. What we brought that was different enabled learning to take place in so many ways. For example, how a son or daughter died was unique to each dad. For some it was the result of a vehicular accident. For others it was due to a misdiagnosis or an act of negligence on the part of someone else. For still others it was because of an illness, an addiction, an act of murder, or a taking of one's own life.

I learned many things from the dads. Each one had something to teach me. And I continue to learn as each one continues to share details of his experience and insights emerging from his reflection. I also learn from the questions that are raised and the varying answers that are given. The differing perspectives lend themselves to a fuller awareness and a more penetrating analysis of what each of us has gone through.

The perspective that I bring is one that looks at the loss of my daughter from a longer time period than anyone else in the group. Her death was on May 11, 1996. A lot has taken place in my life since then. And through those years I have been able to integrate that loss into my life, to reconstruct what gives my life meaning, and to reflect on Bonnie's life as well as her death. I have been able to give thanks for all she became and all she accomplished. And, as a result of my sharing, some dads have indicated that they have been encouraged by seeing that I've made it through the very difficult years that immediately follow the death of a child.

Being part of the Dads Group has also allowed me to reflect on Bonnie's death and the ways I have dealt with it. That is, it has given me the opportunity to reprocess my grief and, in doing so, to gain insight into what I experienced personally, as well as what I experienced through the lives of others—family members, friends, and other acquaintances.

At the very time Bonnie died, and ever since, I have looked for ways that good might come out of our tragedy. My primary motivation in doing so is my belief that God works for good in everything. God doesn't cause a lot of things that happen. They just simply happen. And the reason they happen doesn't have to be determined.

As a result of this belief, my family and I have looked for ways that good might emerge from Bonnie's death. One was the donation of her organs at the time of her death and the successful transplantation of some of those organs. Another was the building of houses with Habitat for Humanity in Indianapolis—known as "Bonnie Builds"—in 1996, and again in 1997, 1998, and 1999. A third is the endowed scholarship that has been established in Bonnie's memory at

DePauw University—one that commemorates her commitment to, and involvement in, winter term service trips—with the earnings providing resources for students to participate in these life-changing experiences. A fourth has been the publication of a book and several articles that I have written. A fifth has been the many invitations I have received to share the story of Bonnie's life and death. And a sixth has been the changed outlook regarding what is really important in life that has taken place in my life and the lives of many others, especially family members and close friends.

Being a part of the Dads Group is also something good that has come out of my tragedy. I probably would never have met—certainly not have come to know—most of the dads in the group. And that is why the group means so much to me.

Friendship—real friendship—is at the core of my connection to the Dads Group. I feel a deep sense of solidarity with each dad in the group. If one of them would call me—for any reason, and at any time of day or night—I would respond. I would listen if he wanted to talk. I would talk if he wanted to listen. Yes, I would go if he asked me to come—any time, any place, for any reason. I would trust him not to take advantage of me. And, what is so encouraging to me, I know if I needed to make a call to one of them, he would do the same for me.

There is a bond between the dads in this group. It runs deep. And it's there to stay—regardless of what happens!

Adolf Hansen

Greg Reed

MARCH 20, 1978 – JUNE 8, 1999

THIS STORY IS BEING WRITTEN NEAR THE NINTH ANNIVERSARY OF the death of my son Greg.

In a lot of respects I wish I could have done this a few years earlier. Not that I have moved on, because you can never do that, but because a lot of the details were more readily available memory-wise. This story is about my son's death, dealing with my grief, and how the Dads Group has helped me in processing and dealing with my grief.

Greg, up to his teenage years, was just about the best son I could have ever hoped for: happy, funny, bright, very athletic, and much focused. But also caring, and loving. One of his biggest achievements was at eleven years old. He tried out for the best travel hockey team in the Chicago area—as a virtually unknown player at the time—and was chosen out of three hundred kids. I was as proud of him for just having the guts to try out as I was for him making the team. One of his best traits was how he would not shy away from trying anything—whether it was swimming, skiing, dirt bike riding, going out for any sport, or trying out for plays and musicals. And Greg never met a stranger. No matter who they were or where they were from, Greg was their friend.

In Greg's early teens he was diagnosed with bipolar disorder. His moods had changed drastically, and all the wonderful things that I just said about Greg began slowly fading away. He never really wanted to accept the diagnosis. He took his meds for a while, but they never made him feel normal. So he quit taking them and started trying alcohol and drugs. He hid it from us very well at first, but we eventually found out and confronted him. He saw many counselors, went to AA and tried a lot of programs. Greg hit bottom around the ages of seventeen and nineteen. But in the summer of 1997, he really started to make great progress in dealing with his addictions. He began working two jobs—one at a pizza place, and another doing landscaping—and was doing so well at the pizza job that they were placing him into the management program. Greg won the "Most Valuable Employee of the Month" award three times at the pizza place in 1998. And he remained clean for approximately eighteen months.

In late April of 1999, one of Greg's close friends died of a heroin overdose. My wife Jackie and I did not see it then, but his friend's death affected Greg greatly. He was living at home at the time, and he was very upset over it, but we did not detect any drug or alcohol use. On Monday, June 7, 1999, Greg came home after work, then went out with his boss for a dinner meeting to discuss the management program. Prior to leaving, Greg and Jackie were doing laundry together. Greg left for the meeting and returned later, letting his mom know he was heading out to Broad Ripple, a local spot for young adults. He left again, but did not come home again that night. Or the next day.

After one day with Greg not coming home, we knew something was wrong. And for him to miss several days, and important family events, was unthinkable. Greg's sister had just graduated from high school and her graduation party was the following Saturday, June 12, 1999. Even though Greg was twenty-one years old, if he were going to stay away, he would leave a message with his sister or one of his friends. He would not miss his sister's graduation party.

We started making calls right away, and tried to put the pieces together.

Several of Greg's friends had said Greg was going to "Carma's" on Monday night, June 7. So, the day after Greg had failed to return home, Jackie contacted Carma and spoke directly with her. Carma denied Greg had ever made it down to her home. Jackie called her several times during the summer, but Carma still said she didn't know anything.

Two weeks after Greg had gone missing, we received a telephone call from High Point law enforcement—in North Carolina. They had found Greg's car being driven by two young thugs who had refused to say where they had gotten the car. They were held in jail for about a week or so and then released. I flew down to High Point and drove Greg's car back to our home.

A friend of Greg's since high school, Neal, came to our house that summer, and gave Jackie a hug ... but said he had no idea where Greg was.

We hung fliers all summer, hoping that someone would give us some information. Through most of the summer I believed Greg was still alive.

Near the end of the summer we started to hear rumors that Greg was gone, but no one ever came forth with the truth.

I never believed in my wildest dreams that Greg had died. The detective on Greg's case, Detective Todd Uhrick, had never informed us of the great possibility that Greg was dead. He at times tried to prepare us, but without any evidence, he decided not to.

On Sunday, September 19, 1999, late in the evening, we received a call from a man who thought he had seen Greg playing basketball at a city park in Indianapolis. The man stated he had gone back to the furniture store where Greg's Missing Persons flier was posted, to be sure it was Greg. This man was almost positive it was our son he had seen. The call came so late Sunday evening that we decided to wait until early Monday morning to pursue it. We were up all night unable to sleep.

The following morning we called Detective Uhrick. Although he had received several unsubstantiated calls that Greg had died, there had been, until then, only two people who had called Crime Stoppers with official statements regarding Greg's case.

My wife, daughter and I drove to the park and spoke with the park ranger, folks at the park, the community center staff, guys playing basketball—anyone we could find—but no one recognized Greg's picture or remembered ever having seen him. We knocked on doors in the area and handed out fliers with Greg's picture and contact information. Still, no one recognized him. As the three of us drove home in silence, we felt so hopeless and lost. Our spirits had been so high the night before and now we were praying for Greg's return.

Later that same evening, I was watching the evening news and there was a segment about the remains of a body that had been discovered in Morgan County.

The camera focused on a pair of boots.

And I knew.

I knew right then the boots were Greg's.

And right then I knew Greg was gone.

I rushed to our bedroom, woke up Jackie and told her I was scared.

Then I told her what I had just heard and seen on the news.

The news report stated that the human remains had been found by two AT&T workers around 2:30 p.m.—the same time we had been pounding on neighborhood homes in the park. One of the workers had stepped away from the tower for a cigarette smoke and just happened to look down and see what she thought were human remains. She called her partner over and they immediately called law enforcement. The news stated the name of the coroner called to the site. We had a copy of Greg's dental film, so Jackie immediately called the Morgan County Sheriff's Department and spoke with the coroner who was still working on the case. The coroner would not confirm at that time with Jackie, but we knew in our hearts it was Greg. We just knew. We held each other and were falling apart. There are no words to describe this moment except for such grief and terror.

The next day Detective Uhrick and his partner came to our home and confirmed our fears with the matching dental records.

We then had to wait another three weeks to have Greg's funeral, because the police had sent samples to the FBI in Washington, DC, to try to determine the cause of death—which never was determined because the remains had been exposed in the open too long. Greg's death certificate states, "Cause of Death: Unknown."

As we waited for the FBI lab results, we were asked to assist Detective Larry Sanders, who had been newly assigned to Greg's case because it was now under the jurisdiction of Morgan County. We continued to question Greg's friends and follow up on every lead we had in order to find out who was responsible. As Detective Sanders received more information from the two individuals who had contacted Crime Stoppers, he determined that Neal, Greg's friend from high school who had come to the house during the summer to console us, and Carma, the woman Jackie had called several times, were involved—along with Carma's boyfriend and partner, Brandon. Neal confessed and told the police the whole story. But the true story will never be known, because everyone involved in the events of that night lied repeatedly to keep themselves from being incriminated in Greg's death.

Evidently that night—the night Greg said he was going to Broad Ripple—two of Greg's old friends, Carma and Brandon, had called him, inviting him to their house, in a town near Bloomington. Greg and Neal then drove down to Carma and Brandon's to buy and use heroin. We will never know what compelled Greg to drive down there and buy drugs, but he did. According to Neal, Carma, and Brandon, Greg was the only one in the group doing drugs. Neal said Greg had not been doing well—that he had been having difficulty breathing and looked really bad. But instead of calling for help, the three decided to do nothing and went to bed. This was around 4 a.m. or so. They claimed that, when they woke up later in the morning, they found Greg dead. At around 11:30 a.m., instead of calling the police, they lifted Greg by his feet and arms and placed him in the back seat of his car and drove around until they found a secluded, remote area to dump Greg's body. I use the word *dump*, because this is the word used by Carma and Brandon after Greg's remains were found in Morgan County, Indiana.

Carma and Brandon were experienced enough in dealing drugs to know that in the county Greg died in, Owen County, the laws are more severe than in Morgan County, where his body was found, for a person dying of an illegal drug overdose. The drug dealer(s) could be charged with murder and face up to twenty-five years in prison. Carma and Brandon were both aware that in Owen County they could be charged with murder. So Neal and Brandon drove around for about two hours with Greg propped up in the back seat of his car, as Carma and her seven-year-old daughter followed in another vehicle. They decided to dump Greg in a wooded area behind a cell phone tower, off of Observatory Road, about forty miles south of Indianapolis. They covered his body with leaves and debris so he wouldn't be found. They told the police that they cleaned the inside and outside of Greg's car, then drove to Indianapolis and left the car in the Broad Ripple area. But the car was found in High Point, North Carolina, so the detectives believed that Carma and Brandon really drove Greg's car to North Carolina and abandoned it there.

Keep in mind, these were people Greg had considered friends. We were stunned that they had gone to such disturbing lengths to conceal the truth—and to hide Greg's death.

Once Greg's body was found, and the story was revealed, Neal, Carma and Brandon were arrested.

The court proceedings took nearly one year to complete.

Carma and Brandon received one year in jail.

Neal received ninety days probation.

Quite often when trials and/or investigations are involved after a child's death, the total focus is on the proceedings of the trial or investigations, and not on dealing or coping with the grief. In a lot of respects you want to avoid dealing with it altogether, hoping that, by the end of the trial, the intensity of the grief or loss will have somehow lessened to a point that you will be able to go on with your life to some extent. But it's once the trial and investigations are over that the real challenge of dealing with the loss begins.

My emotions ran the gambit. I felt hopeless, betrayed. I felt like a failure to Greg, myself, and my family. I was mad at or about everything. I was mad at Greg for being selfish and stupid, mad at myself for not being aware that Greg was sliding backwards again, mad about not helping him to avoid what he had done. Mad at the people asking me if I was over it yet, mad at relatives for not trying to understand how I felt.

I went through all the what ifs and why didn'ts and, after months and months of beating myself up, I came to the realization that I had to find a way to physically and mentally carry on.

Early on I felt physically weak as well as mentally weak. As a father and a husband I felt I was the one who must lead the family back to some kind of normalcy. I thought, "If the family sees me going through some of the old routines, it will help them get back into their old routines." What I found out, however, was that my old routines and life would never be the same. The sooner a dad who has lost a child realizes and faces this, the quicker he will be on the road to healing.

One of the most recurring themes in our stories is that, in the grief or healing process, you do whatever you have to do to survive. What I mean by that is, if you do not want to go to family functions, holidays, etc., you really don't have to go. If you know that you will not be able to get through the gathering, then disregard everyone else's opinions, and *don't go*. In most cases no one else has walked in your shoes. They don't have a clue what you are going through. So when they try to lay the guilt trips on you about how your absence makes everyone else feel sad, they need to get a grip.

That comes to the other recurring theme in our stories: for the most part, most friends and family DON'T "GET IT." It is not a slam, but because all people have lost, or will lose, parents, grandparents, even spouses, they often think they understand what you are going through. But again, really, they don't have a clue. It is the same as I have no idea what it would be like to raise a child with a debilitating disease. I can imagine what it might be like, but I have not lived it, so I really could not and would not advise the parents on how to deal with their feelings.

For quite a while after my son's death, I felt one to two steps slower than the rest of the world. It takes years to get back in a new rhythm of life. You have to go back to work fairly soon and pretend that life goes on, but inside you try to get through each day one at a time.

I came to the Dads Group in May of 2004, as one of the early members. I, too, am a member of St. Luke's United Methodist Church, and Marsha Hutchinson, a pastor at the church, told me of this group that had just started up and why not check it out. It had been several years since I had been to any counseling or grief group meetings and I thought it would be good to meet with dads who were in the same boat that I was in.

I connected with everyone immediately. What I really appreciated right off was the total honesty in how they felt and their thought process in dealing with current situations. You know it's something special when four complete strangers are telling each other how they are trying to cope with the world after losing one of the most precious people they will ever know in their lives.

What I learned very fast was that, for the most part, we all felt and dealt with life close to the same—and that was very reassuring, to know that I was not some far-off thinking dad who was out of touch with reality. I had finally found other people who "GOT IT." I had found a group that, if I wanted to talk all morning about something that was heavy on my mind, I could do so and that would be okay; and if I just sat there and said nothing, that would be okay, too. What we soon learned was that there was no one there to judge us on how we should think or react to situations, but that, if we were looking for advice, there was always someone who could tell us what they had done in a similar circumstance. It does not mean their solution was right or wrong, but it was an option on how we might deal with it ourselves.

This group is a place where everyone comes carrying a heavy load over their shoulder, and by the time they leave, their load does not feel near as heavy as when they came in. It seems to have been dispersed among the group. Within a few months of joining the group, I saw the anger in myself subside. It seemed that I was more concerned with the well-being of the other dads than with my own well-being. You don't forget why you're there, but your focus is more on other dads and less on yourself. It seemed that after I joined, there were three or four others who joined soon after me, and the focus was on getting the new dads to feel at home and to know that they had come to the right place. I feel that I have a responsibility to pass on the coping skills and enlightenment that I have learned and received by coming to the group.

Some of my other friends have asked me how long I think I will need the group, and I say, "As long as the group lasts." We have developed such a strong bond, that leaving never really crosses my mind. After nine years I am still grieving. The pain is no longer raw, but the sadness never really goes away. It's always right under the skin.

One of the reasons I'm writing this story is to help dads who have not had the opportunity to be in such a group, and who haven't been able to discuss the way they feel—one, three, eight or eleven years after losing their child—to get a feeling of the ways that many of us, who are walking in their shoes, are dealing with our grief. I think there are a lot of dads out there who, after a few years go by, feel the subject of the loss of their child should be buried along with their child, and I disagree.

The group provides a forum for us to discuss very difficult personal questions with other men who sincerely care for our well-being. But this connection isn't all about grief. We have way more laughs than tears at our meetings.

One of our group sayings is that we are all in the group that no one wants to belong to. Ironically, without being in this group, I never would have known some of the best friends I have ever had.

Steve Reed

Jake Laird

SEPTEMBER 17, 1972 – AUGUST 18, 2004

ON A SUNNY JULY AFTERNOON IN 2004, I WAS STANDING ON THE number three tee station at a local golf course with my friend Tom Harford. Tom had just experienced, in March, the loss of his oldest son Karl to a tragic shooting incident while at college. I remember Tom being so quiet for such a long time. I finally approached him and told him, "I can't imagine what you're going through, and I don't know if I could ever handle it if something like that happened to one of my boys." I wanted to let him know that if he ever wanted to just talk I would be there. Little did I know Tom would be at my front door a few months later offering me the same comfort.

August 18, 2004: A date etched in my mind forever.

August 18, 2004, started out in a usual way with my wife, Debbie, not being able to sleep. I heard her get up out of bed, and looked at the clock. It was 4:30. I rolled back over, knowing I had a couple hours until she would wake me for work.

At 5:05 my life was changed forever. I was awakened by Debbie yelling, "Mike there is a policeman at the front door and I am not going to answer it!" I immediately jumped out of bed, scrambled to put on my shirt and pants, and all the time my mind was trying to figure out what was going on. Why would a policeman be at our door this early in the morning? Thoughts of something happening to my youngest son, Gabe, stationed in the army in Germany, raced through my head. I heard Debbie open the door, and as I hit the second step of the stairs I heard the words that will be etched into my mind forever, when she screamed, "No, not my Jake!" As I reached the bottom step I saw my wife being held by a chaplain from the local police department, and a uniformed patrolman beside them. As I ran to Debbie and held her, the police officer told me our son Jake, an Indianapolis policeman, had been shot and killed on the south side of Indianapolis. He explained that Jake had answered a 911 call, and that he and four other police officers had been shot by an assailant with an SKS rifle. As I asked question after question he told me Jake was the only fatality of the officers. Yes, the assailant was dead, but he had no other details.

They then wanted to escort us down to Wishard Hospital in Indianapolis where Jake had been taken. I told them we would meet them there. It was at this time, as I was getting dressed and helping Debbie, that I suddenly found myself going into what I call the "patriarchal protective mode." A million thoughts raced through my mind: how do I help my wife, how could this happen, what about Jake's little girl, I need to call my other two sons, my folks, my wife's folks and other relatives. Debbie and I both made a few phone calls on the way to the hospital to notify people before it was on the news that morning.

When we arrived at the hospital, we were met by a man named Jerry Baker. Little did I know that this man would eventually become an integral part of my life. He led us down a hallway which was lined on both sides with police officers all crying and reaching out to touch and comfort us. At the end of the hall was a curtain leading into a huge room. When we entered the room, they had Jake laying on a gurney covered with sheets. He had absolutely no marks on him. The doctors told us he had been shot one time in the shoulder, an inch from his protective vest. The bullet had ricocheted off his collar bone and deflected downward through his heart and liver, exiting through his back.

We stayed with Jake as other members of the family showed up to offer us support and pay their respects, including our oldest son, Chris, who was a Union County Deputy Sheriff.

Indianapolis Mayor Bart Peterson and Marion County Prosecutor Carl Brizzi greeted us and offered their condolences before we were escorted to a receiving room in the hospital where numerous police officers came by to make sure we were alright.

It was at this time the chief of police took me into a private room and explained to me in very specific details what had occurred that morning. Several fearful neighbors had called 911 to report that a man was running rampant through the area, shooting at houses with an assault rifle. We were told that when Jake heard the dispatcher, and his fellow police friend screaming over the radio that he had been shot, he didn't hesitate for even a second to run to his aid. Sixteen minutes later, four police officers lay wounded, and Jake and the killer were dead. It was determined subsequently that the killer had, earlier, also shot and killed his mother.

As I went back into the receiving room I looked at my watch and realized it was time to call our youngest son, Gabe, who was stationed in Germany in the U.S. Army and was nine hours ahead of us in time. That call was the hardest phone call I have ever made in my life. To tell him we had lost his older brother, and not be able to be there to tell him in person, and help comfort him, was extremely upsetting. The Army and American Red Cross had him home in twenty-four hours.

When I returned to my wife, people were asking us a thousand questions. We realized the family needed to meet with the police crisis team and make arrangements. I made the suggestion for everyone to meet at our house that afternoon. As everyone left, my wife and I went down to see Jake one more time before we left. The police department had an officer standing guard over our son. It was politely explained that they would always have at least one officer at Jake's side twenty-four hours a day, as respect for one of their brothers who had fallen in the line of duty.

That afternoon was the start of five days of unbelievable events. Decisions were made by the crisis team where to have the funeral, where to have the calling, who would pick up relatives at the airport, who would handle the media, etc. They also arranged hotel rooms for out-of-state relatives. There must have been a hundred details for us to decide. I had no idea what was in store for us. It was totally incredible. I tried to shortstop most plans and questions myself, to avoid having my wife experience any more pain than she was dealing with already; but the police department and the crisis team made all arrangements—setting up visitation, flowers, the funeral service, honor guard, and several other details. They were making sure Jake was being honored as a hero who had given his life for the city of Indianapolis. Plans were being made for two thousand police officers from all over the country to be in attendance.

When everyone left that evening, it was the first time my wife and I had time alone. The reality finally sunk in. We had just lost our son.

The next morning was the start of a new whirlwind of events. Friends and neighbors stopped by with food and support. The phone never quit ringing. Our next-door neighbor fielded phone messages and took control of telling us both what we needed to do and what time to do it.

The local media TV stations set up remotes in our yard and wanted interviews. Details of the funeral service needed to be finalized. We also needed to arrange for our son Gabe to be picked up at the airport, as it was a top priority for us to be there when he landed. I knew that was going to be a very sad moment.

The calling was held at Crown Hill Cemetery with full police honors displayed. We were told to expect several hours of people visiting. It started at 1 p.m. and ended at 9 p.m. The visitation line for people to honor our son was sometimes two hours long. There were friends, police officers from several different cities and states, politicians, and complete strangers coming in to show honor and respect to Jake. It touched our hearts that people cared so much.

The funeral was held at St. Luke's United Methodist Church. Several speakers and friends spoke with reverence for Jake. The church was completely filled and had an over-flow into several extra rooms with television feeds. A procession of over five hundred police vehicles proceeded to take a route through the city and pass by Jake's south side police station. The whole route was lined with people holding signs or bowing their heads. It was quite a tribute to Jake and our family. The burial was at Crown Hill Cemetery with full honor guard and bagpipes in front of a caisson carrying Jake to his resting place in the Fallen Heroes section of Crown Hill. As the funeral services ended, every police officer in attendance passed by and placed a carnation on his casket as a tribute to their fallen brother.

As everyone left the cemetery, I remember standing at the casket with Deb, and again realizing our son Jake was really gone.

The next few weeks were long and hard. I kept thinking about Jake as a kid growing up. I remembered the days we played pitch and catch, coaching his baseball team, helping him with his paper route, teaching him how to shave. I remembered him getting his first "real job" at a fast food restaurant. I thought about teaching him how to drive and the first car I helped him buy. (It was so important for him to show me he could make the payments on his own. He did and never missed one.) I kept thinking about how he talked to me about becoming a marine and how, after three weeks of boot camp, he called and said, "Dad please get me out of this and I will do anything you ask." I remembered telling him to just hang in there and he would be fine. Eight years later this marine sergeant was calling me again and wanting to talk about joining the Indianapolis Police Department. Again I promised him I would help him any way I could if that was what he wanted to do. I was able to have a couple people write recommendation letters for Jake, and he proceeded to start on his ultimate dream job adventure.

Jake and I solved a lot of problems together, which is a reward for being a parent. I didn't realize it at the time, but my biggest challenge in facing this tragedy of losing my son, was going to be that, for the first time, neither Jake nor I were going to be able to fix this problem. This feeling has been the main reason for my grief. It has become the main focus in my life in dealing with this loss. It is something I rarely ever talk about, and keep inside of myself to deal with. A father should never have to bury his son. It still bothers me to this day that, as Jake's dad, I couldn't have somehow protected him.

I AM NOT ALONE.

For the next couple of weeks I tried to keep my emotions in check for my wife and the family. Deep inside I was feeling like my heart was half gone. My desire to work was never there for a very long time. I was fortunate to own my business and have a very capable manager to run the store. When I was there I didn't stay long. At home I tried to be there for my wife as she needed me. I realized then that men and women grieve very differently.

The gentleman who had virtually become my shadow during all this tragedy, Jerry Baker, was very familiar with how I was feeling. He had lost his son a couple years earlier. His son Jason had also been in law enforcement, and had been shot in the line of duty, as well. About four weeks after Jake's death, Jerry asked me if I would be interested in going to a meeting that he attended with other dads who had lost children. At first I did not want to participate. I felt it was not something that was going to help me, especially in the frame of mind I was in.

But eventually I went. I was sure this would be a waste of time. What could these people help me with? They could not possibly understand what and how I was feeling. The first meeting, I met five individuals who went around the table and related to me their "stories." I listened very carefully to each one of them. Their stories were all different but had one common theme: they had lost their son or daughter. And I immediately realized, I am not alone. Their stories touched me, and as strange as it seems, I felt myself feeling for them and almost making my situation with Jake a secondary problem for me. They asked me to relate my story if I wanted to, but most of them already knew a lot of it because of all the publicity it had received in the media. I tried to tell as much as I could before I broke down and started sobbing. These strangers never said a thing. Each one got up and gave me a pat on the back, or a hug, and told me it was okay to cry. For, you see, these guys had been through this same day before. They truly understood. I didn't say much more that day, but I listened very intently about how they handled their feelings and situations that would arise unexpectedly. I left that first day with assurance that I truly was not alone.

The next few weeks it was still hard for me at the meetings. I never left without having tears in my eyes. As I continued to participate and share my feelings with these new "friends," the meetings became a necessity for me to attend. I began to look forward to Tuesday mornings. The common thread that we shared, with the loss of our children, made it so easy to relate to the way I was feeling. The blessing I had received from these gentlemen was the fact that their experiences were on different levels of years since they had lost their children. My benefit was that they had already been where I was now, and where I was proceeding to go. Each one could share what his feelings had been at that same point, as I progressed on my journey of time.

After a few months, I asked my friend Tom Harford to come and check out this unbelievable group of men I met with on Tuesday mornings. He told me he would come and see what it was like. Two years, and we're still meeting these gentlemen.

Unfortunately, it is a group that keeps getting bigger. More dads keep coming, which means more dads are losing their children. I have met men of various backgrounds and occupations that I probably would never have met, had it not been for our common thread of tragedy.

One day I was talking to a customer in my store right after one of my Tuesday meetings, and she inquired what we were all about. As I explained to her what it was we did, she asked me if I would call her boyfriend and invite him to the group, as he had just lost his daughter recently. Needless to say, Anthony has become a member and a new friend. I have developed several new friendships with these guys. We play golf, go to baseball games together, and occasionally have dinner parties with our spouses.

Without realizing, I was slowly coming back to some sort of normalcy. I know I will never be the same man I was before we lost Jake, but in some respects his death has made me a better man. Things that I took for granted in the past, I realize now are important parts in my life that should be treasured and not forgotten. My feelings are easier to accept, and I don't find it so hard to express them as I used to in the past. I have become much closer to God, and prayer has become a daily part of my life again.

Each and every day, I still think about Jake and always wonder what he would be doing about this or how would he have liked that. I think of all the fun he would be having with his daughter Kaylee, his true pride and joy. There is always that tear in my eye at those times, but I now know that's okay.

I will always miss Jake. I know that he was a good boy who grew into a very courageous hero as a young man.

At this very moment, Jake is happy and content, and all of those dreams of his, they are a reality. You see, Jake has seen the face of God. Jake not only knows, but understands, the plan God had for him. He knows why he died so young. Jake has all of the answers to all of my questions. I also know God has that boy, marine, police officer, father, and son with Him now, and that someday I will get to see Jake again.

Out of tragedy sometimes there comes good.

Jake's death has brought many positive changes.

Deb and I saw the Jake Laird bill #1776 pass the Indiana House and Senate. When Governor Mitch Daniels signed this bill into action, Indiana laws changed. The criteria used to return weapons that have been seized, now make it much more difficult for someone with a history of mental illness—who has been arrested or detained, and subsequently released from jail or a mental health facility—to obtain their weapons again. Jake's assailant had a previous history of mental illness. He had spent some time in a mental institution and, when he was released, the police had no recourse other than to return his guns back to him, because it was the law.

Debbie and I have created The Jake Laird Memorial Fund, which offers financial assistance to any public safety individual enduring financial hardships due to injuries incurred while on duty. It also provides monies for new equipment or the institution of new programs. We have an annual golf tourney as our only fundraiser each year to raise money for this fund. What started as an event with eighty golfers the first year, has grown into an event of over three hundred golfers last year. Several corporations have helped in the sponsorship of the outing. As of 2008, we have been able to donate over $80,000 to various police and firefighter causes throughout the state of Indiana.

Who would have thought so many police officers' and fire fighters' families, and so many children from city community days, would be able to feel hope as a result of the death of our son?

You really *can* turn disappointment into something good.

In closing, I ask anyone who reads my story to take a look at your own life, your joys, your sorrows, and try to turn those disappointments into something good.

Don't allow yourself to stay in a place of despair and sadness. You may miss what God has planned for you as a result of a tragedy.

Remember to try to seek out others who are experiencing a similar situation as you are. I really do believe there is strength in numbers. Sharing feelings openly with others, and not keeping them bottled up inside of you, will provide you some comfort in dealing with your loss.

I hope my story will help you in some small way, in coping with your situation.

Thank you and God bless each of you.

Mike Laird

Jennifer "Jenny" Nicole Dodds

JULY 13, 1979 – JUNE 16, 2001

IN JUNE, 2001, I WAS LIVING AN ALMOST IDEAL LIFE: UPSCALE middle class neighborhood with white picket fence and two English Spaniels, two-career family income, three kids who had made it into their twenties without car injuries or legal issues and who managed substance abuse pressure well. My wife Reyna and I were in the relatively economically stable healthcare field. Both sides of parents were reasonably healthy. My dad was showing signs of advanced aging, but otherwise all were very active. For that matter, I had not lost a single immediate family member in my then fifty-four years of life.

The family life was full of major events and growth. Our son Mark was living at home after graduating from the University of Texas with his dual undergraduate degrees. Our youngest daughter, Jenny, was living at home with her dog, going to school at IUPUI, studying business and working. Tiffani, our oldest, and Dave, her husband, were establishing a life in Orlando, having been married at a big family affair in the summer of 2000.

Beyond career, family was my attention, and Reyna my best friend. My typical non-family interaction was work-related, with no participation in organized groups.

Reyna and I felt like our lives had been blessed with few life challenges. However, Reyna, more than I, had become concerned with Jenny's high blood pressure and complaints of palpitations and fatigue. See, my priorities were on my stagnating career growth that had peaked to a point where I seemed unable to achieve a promotion. My priority was working hard, being the expert, and leveraging my technical knowledge in science and my almost twenty-one years of on the job business-gained acumen. Essentially, my priorities were dead center in work and doing what I thought it took to gain more success by typical success standards, even though I was falling short.

Outside of work, which honestly had my full attention, I was only going through life, not as engaged in the family as much as they would've liked and, retrospectively, not living life to its fullest.

Jenny complained of fatigue, racing heart and generally not feeling well to our family physician. He referred her to a cardiologist who adjusted her blood pressure medicine, ran some tests, noted her atypical midriff growth and lack of controlled blood pressure, but assured us that she had no heart problems. On June 15, 2001, Jenny called Reyna and was not feeling well and Reyna then asked a neighbor to take her to the hospital to avoid any delays. Jenny was feeling arm pain, chest pain, racing heart, and was more fatigued than usual. Reyna called the cardiologist's office and was advised that Jenny should go to the hospital where he was on call. Our neighbor took Jenny to the emergency room. I finished my business at work and leisurely drove to the hospital believing that the trained professionals I was around in my career would take proper care of my daughter. The ER physician ordered some basic tests, conferred with the cardiologist, and jointly decided she did not have a heart problem. We asked for more specific tests, but were again reassured they were not necessary. The physicians agreed she was suffering from anxiety, and that it was not likely her symptoms were related to cardiovascular disease. We believed them since she had been an avid soccer player in high school, homecoming queen her senior high school year, and was now a young woman going to college, working where I worked, and living at home. At twenty-one, anxiety and stress were possible causes—not heart problems.

Jenny had matured into a deeply living life-rooted woman, partly through her life experiences of being adventurous. She had gone from not wanting to get her hands dirty, to crawling under a house to help build a foundation in the Appalachian Mountains for a Barrington, Illinois, church project. At home, she had grown from rolling her eyes at everything Reyna said, to having Reyna as friend and confidante. She was showing her love for others, and others showed their appreciation for her, as well. At school, Jenny was amazed that she was selected to be homecoming queen the first year of her new school opening. In her unassuming way, she shared with us her perception that, even though she was not the prettiest girl in the high school, people must have liked her.

From the day it seems she skipped crawling, and went from the baby bed to walking, Jenny refused to let obstacles get in her way, but instead found a way to overcome the obstacles. She typically had a high level of energy and get-it-done attitude, so we were worried about her unusual fatigue. We were relieved her symptoms were not cardiovascular-related, and thought that maybe they were due to her Poly Cystic Ovarian Syndrome, which had been diagnosed in mid 2000, or hormone imbalance. To pursue it further, Reyna planned to make an appointment with another specialist the following week.

The next morning, Jenny got up early, unusual for a weekend, and asked me to prepare her favorite breakfast. It was Saturday, June 16, following her ER visit and the day before Father's Day. We ate on the patio on a beautiful sunny day. After breakfast, I went to the task of finding out what was wrong with the dishwasher. Jenny sat on the couch, began to sweat, felt the palpitations, and was exceedingly tired, even though she had just gotten up from sleeping. She decided to go to the basement to cool off. Within less than two minutes, her dog followed her to the basement and began to bark wildly. I went downstairs to find Jenny unconscious, not responding and lifeless. I tried CPR but failed. Reyna called 911 and we frantically waited for them to arrive.

The ambulance team tried to revive her, and asked me to leave the basement. Here I was leaving my youngest child there and letting others try to do what most dads feel is their duty: "save their child." Having tried several times to restart her heart, they brought Jenny up in a gurney and took her and my wife in the ambulance to another hospital. Jenny was pronounced dead on arrival at approximately 8 a.m., within about an hour since we had shared breakfast.

Before leaving for the hospital, the sheriff's department asked about any arguments or abusive behavior on my part or other family members—a normal question following a sudden death at home. Of course not, this was Camelot until about 8 a.m. and I was the man protecting those from harm in Camelot.

I recall still being coherent as I drove behind the ambulance to the hospital. However, the feeling of helplessness again returned—the first when I could not revive her, and now as I realized the siren was not blaring as it traveled to another hospital in the community.

At the hospital, my realization that I no longer was in control of the situation began, and I, the problem-solver of the house, could not fix this situation like I had been trying to do earlier that morning with the dishwasher. The numbness and foggy mind began then, as I felt that this could not be happening. I will surely wake up and realize the emergency room physician that was standing there with tears in his eyes, the hospital chaplain also in tears, and our own minister, were not talking about Jenny, our youngest child.

We later found from the autopsy, dictated by her death at home, that two of her arteries were over ninety percent blocked. There was no indication of the typical medical assumption that, at her age, substance abuse had caused her sudden cardiac arrest. She died at twenty-one because her heart stopped. Jenny was the first to die in our family, before Reyna and I, before her grandparents and aunts and uncles.

This foggy mind continued through 9/11 as I recall realizing the tragedy but felt disconnected with the enormity of the loss. This disconnection with life around me continued for well over a year as I tried to find a way to live a life devoid of my youngest child.

About two years later, Reyna asked me if I was interested in meeting with a group of men on Tuesday morning for breakfast at a local restaurant. This group was unique in that all of the men had lost children unexpectedly and generally without warning. I said I would go once, but I was not sure I wanted to do so routinely. I went because, even though I had spent a year or so on anti-depressants and in counseling—with both couples groups and in private sessions—I knew I did not seem to be making the kind of progress that would allow me to function productively during the rest of my life journey with her loss. Reyna and I had worked hard to keep our relationship strong throughout and to share our feelings, which often were at opposite levels of grieving. We knew Jenny would have wanted that, and this was probably the first time we began to measure our actions according to what Jenny would have wanted. However, I knew I was still struggling as exemplified by the fact that I was continuing to go through the motions at work and not feeling truly engaged in life.

When I met the group of six other men that morning, we shared the stories of our individual loss—as the group, now sixteen, always does when a new man comes to his first breakfast. I was struck by the stories of the other guys who in my mind had stories more devastating and heartwrenching as a parent than my own. We shared stories about the tears, the anger, the helplessness and the fact that life is not supposed to be this way, as we are supposed to die before our children. We discussed moving through the day as if we were in slow motion and the outside world were nonexistent. When I went home that night I told Reyna that not only did I want to go back, I wanted to avoid missing a single week.

Thereafter, I booked my work calendar with time to come into the office later each Tuesday morning. I also realized that my "progress" in this journey was not unlike my new unlikely friends'—friends I would never have known were it not for the circumstances that brought men from different paths in life together—and that my unusual feelings and reactions to my environment were not unique to me alone. The previously big things and irritations in life seemed so small now, and the previously smaller things like laughing seemed to be big events.

Through the next three years, the group shared deeper feelings of change in priorities in life. Work became a means to an end for many of us, providing us the means to support the legacy of our children. The means to finance this book. I learned that my moments of uncontrollable outbursts of tears and emotions when alone, like driving in the car, were not uncommon. We also realized that until one has experienced a loss like ours, one cannot "get it." Neither can our colleagues, friends, and often, family. We shared that, in many cases, those we had felt close to before our loss had trouble dealing with our progress in the journey, thinking we should be over it by now. Sometimes our previous friendships changed. Other shared experiences seemed to resonate with all of us in this group who "get it."

We share similar experiences such as when people try to say the right thing like, "well you do have other children," "why did you take her to that hospital?" "your child is in a better place," and agree that this doesn't help at all. However, people wanting to share their thoughts by reaching out and saying something do most often help, and we hope those wanting to relate try to overcome any fear of bringing up the loss. In our case, there was a colleague at work, I barely knew, who overcame the fear of rejection and saying the wrong things. He and his wife called to see if they could stop by and bring us some dinner days after the mourning following the funeral. Their concern and our conversation not only helped at the time, but they have become the dearest of friends, and one of the positive results of that period in our life.

It is only after losing Jenny that I have learned how to overcome the reluctance to reach out. Those who want to reach out can be assured that, in showing their concern, they are not awakening a reminder of the loss since, we all hope, it is never gone. They are not bringing up something that we are not already reminded of frequently. In a song, in a phrase, in a way a person looks, in many small ways. Only "problem-solving" phrases like those mentioned above do not help; however, we all often benefit from the inquiry on how we are doing. Sometimes we share the inner feelings with others, most times not. This is why the Tuesday group is so key to my continued living with this catastrophic change. It's because they get it.

We also know that others often want to move along and often bring us along with them. We do go through life, but feeling different than many, as all of us in the group have that big gut-wrenching void in our hearts, maybe less frequently as time passes, but it is still there as vivid as the days we lost our children.

Every holiday season, we in the group share our struggles with what to do for the holidays. Whether to celebrate, or not. Whether to stay at home, travel, be with family, be with close friends. Whether to be alone. All finding our way through these times where the loss is often most apparent. I have learned from the guys that whatever I feel, I should "go with it," and I know at least one of them has been there and done that.

We also share stories of how we remember our lost kids on their birthday and/or the day of their death. Most of us take the day off from work and do things our children would have done. Reyna and I always go out and buy needed things for the Humane Society, as Jenny was a regular adopter of dogs from the Society. They are given in her name for those dogs she loved so much. On her birthday, July 13, we have a picnic lunch at her gravesite and talk to her. See Jenny always loved to talk.

One commonality of many in the group is a desire to turn the loss into something positive in honor of our lost loved one. Golf outings, 5K runs and walks, scholarships, community support of the less fortunate and, in my case, active engagement in the American Heart Association's efforts to educate and increase the awareness of women, young and not as young, about heart disease as the number one killer of women. Each of us do such things in honor of our lost child. Through the group I also have learned what living life is at a deeper spiritual level. You see this Tuesday morning group is a safe place without judgment, without quick solutions offered, and without pity, where we often relate where we are in our faith journey.

Since the end of the Dodds Camelot life in Carmel, Indiana, in 2001, Reyna and I have experienced many life challenges, but Jenny's loss has helped us live life as she did—to its fullest with enthusiasm, even under these circumstances. I have learned to live Jenny's favorite quote—a discovery we made after her passing while looking through her high school senior year book: "Don't let obstacles get in the way of your dreams, let your dreams get in the way of your obstacles." I have learned to be engaged, passionate about what I do, and informed as an activist—all traits that reflect Jenny's impact on me, and on others. Those who knew Jenny best knew of her special traits, too. Jenny's gravesite memorial is a bench with the inscription "Jenny's passion for life" and words, contributed by friends, describing how others outside of the family saw Jenny: Loving, Elegant, Devoted, Charming, Informed, Polite, Proud, Spirited, Activist.

We continue to live in the same house and live with the memories. My career is still where it was. However, I have been given the opportunity at work to focus on a heart disease project that combines my personal passion, due to Jenny's loss, and my professional passion to make a difference in Jenny's memory. We now have only two living children and are very blessed with a grandson. Reyna and I have lost our fathers. Reyna has been diagnosed with two cancers and treated successfully.

My group of friends who meet on Tuesday mornings have allowed me to share all of these life experiences, feelings, and reactions with them. Including the joy and the grieving. No judgment, no attempt to solve the issue, no suggestion that I should not feel that way, no pity, no undue discomfort at what I share, just listening, nodding and occasionally remembering a similar moment, with laughter or tears.

Through the group, I have learned how to embrace my emotions and feelings and care more about people. Because of the group, I am now engaged in my life. I now feel my life can have a meaning, often in Jenny's memory.

Now, I open this unique group up to others who have unexpectedly lost a child or children, with the realization that many will hesitate to join or will wait until the right time. Like I did. When the time comes, you will know it is worth attending one morning to see if a group like this one helps you through this journey.

I never imagined I would lose a child, or subsequently write a chapter in a book about the loss. But because of the experience of the group, and with a dedication to Jenny's life, I hope truly that each of you reading this chapter find a group, or help start one like our Tuesday morning group.

Jim Dodds

Karl Harford

JANUARY 11, 1984 – MARCH 7, 2004

ON SUNDAY, FEBRUARY 29, 2004, MY WIFE LIVIA AND I DECIDED TO visit our two sons at Ball State University in Muncie, Indiana. Karl was a 20-year-old sophomore, and Brian an 18-year-old freshman. Livia and I were trying to adjust to being empty-nesters. We had mixed emotions about both of our sons now living away at college. Sometimes the quiet around the house was nice, but we also missed them very much.

We drove up after church and arrived in Muncie about 1:00. We decided to go out for lunch at the IHOP close to Karl's apartment. Of course after lunch we had to go to the grocery store, because their mom thought they might go hungry if we didn't fill up the refrigerators. I was planning to go to Alabama for a golf trip with my twin brother, Ted, and six other friends the next week, so I asked Karl if I could borrow his poker chips to take with me for evening entertainment. "Of course," he said, "just don't lose them." After a short visit and a couple of nice hugs we were on our way home. How could I possibly have known this would be the last time I would see Karl?

The golf trip was fantastic and the weather was perfect—70 degrees every day. Ted and I had just turned fifty in February, and we are both golf nuts. I took Ted to the airport in Prattville, Alabama, on Sunday, March 7, at about 6:30 a.m. Then my golf buddies and I drove back to Indiana. We arrived back home about 4 p.m., and I was ready for a slow evening watching basketball on TV.

That evening around 10:00, as Livia and I were about to go to bed, there was a knock on the front door. I opened the door, and there stood two Carmel policemen and a police chaplain. They identified themselves and asked if they could come in. I said sure and immediately asked if one of my sons was hurt or in trouble. I was told to get my wife in here and for us to sit down. We were both shaking already. The officers then asked, "Do you have a son, Karl Harford?" We said yes. Then he said, "There is no easy way to say this. Karl was found in the back seat of his car with a gunshot in his left temple. He is dead." By now I was shaking so hard I wasn't sure what to do. I asked several times, "Are you sure this is our Karl?" They explained that Karl had been to an off-campus party in Muncie (three blocks off campus), and had given a ride home to three strangers he had just met that evening. He never returned, and was found about 8 or 9 a.m. on Sunday. The time of death was estimated at 6 a.m., which was about the time I was taking my brother Ted to the Prattville airport. Livia had been home alone while I was in Alabama—and had almost gone to Muncie, with her sister Teresa, to visit Karl and Brian that Sunday afternoon! We always wondered what would have happened if the police had either come to our house before I had returned from Alabama, or if Livia had gone up to Muncie that day.

Karl's roommates had identified him later Sunday afternoon. The chaplain asked if there was anyone we could call like a minister or a neighbor. We gave him Father Kevin Haines' number; he called, and Father Kevin came right over. Father Kevin is our priest at St. Maria Goretti Parish in Westfield. We have been members at St. Maria Goretti for about ten years, and Livia has taught third or fourth grade there since they opened the school in 1996. I told Livia, "We have to go get Brian, NOW." The officer said Brian, who had been at the party also, was waiting at the police station for us to come and get him. Brian had been too upset to call us himself.

When Father Kevin arrived, Father, Livia, and I all headed for Muncie. I was told I shouldn't drive, but I did and then Father Kevin drove back. We were all calling work and family on cell phones, and we prayed the rosary on the way to Muncie. It was the first time I had been to the Muncie police station, but we found it alright. When we arrived there, Brian was a mess. The officers explained a little more, and I remember Brian saying, "I don't think those guys he took home were bad. They seemed nice." I asked to see Karl, but he was being prepared for an autopsy at a hospital across town, and we needed to get everyone home. We stopped at the dorm, got some of Brian's clothes, and headed back to Carmel.

I found out later that, when Karl was not at his apartment or the house where the party was, his friends had reported him missing to the Muncie Police Department. I think that was around 1 or 2 p.m. Sunday afternoon. Later, Karl's friends and roommates were asked to gather at Karl's apartment to answer questions for the Muncie police. One of the boys had a video of part of the party, and the police took that and asked them all to come to the police station to look at mug shots. They were able to identify all three suspects, and the Muncie and state police began looking for the suspects immediately.

Neither Livia nor I got much sleep that Sunday night. I remember looking out the window Monday morning at all the cars going down the street on their way to work. I thought to myself, "Where are all those people going? Don't they know the world just ended yesterday?" On Monday morning, it hit the TV and newspapers. We were getting calls from both TV and newspaper reporters, asking for interviews. We just had no idea what to say, or what would be printed or shown on TV, so we refused to talk to the reporters, and asked to be left alone to grieve.

There were many SMG parishioners, including Livia's former and present school parents and friends, who came by the house the whole week, bringing enough food to feed an army. Livia's sister from Canada and all her family, my brothers from Indy, Lafayette, California, and Cincinnati— all came within a few days.

Two of the three suspects—an 18-year-old and a 14-year-old—turned themselves in on Tuesday, March 9. They were both charged with adult murder. The third suspect, a 22-year-old, was identified by the other two suspects as the shooter. The 22-year-old suspect fled Muncie and was caught by U.S. Marshals in Indianapolis, on March 19, and charged with six counts including murder. All three suspects were held in the Muncie jail without bond. Evidence showed that, once Karl drove the three suspects to an abandoned home they had directed him to, they pulled out a gun and robbed him of two dollars. At some point a fight broke out. Karl was not a fighter, so I presume the three suspects threatened his life, if he didn't have more money. Three against one is not very good odds. The fight ended when the 22-year-old shot Karl with a single bullet to the left temple. The autopsy showed that the gun was pinned against Karl's head when he was shot. The suspects then shoved Karl's body in the back seat of his car and drove off. Nobody knows where they were taking Karl, because they drove into a utility box in an alley a short ways away and fled the scene.

I was mad at these guys and thought a public hanging would be most fitting for all three of them. When I found out about the 22-year-old suspect's previous arrest in July of 2003, the fact that he was a convicted felon, and that there were warrants out on him for not showing up in court, I was even angrier. Why wasn't this prolific criminal in JAIL!!!???

The group of friends Karl had at BSU, along with Ball State faculty, organized a candlelight vigil ceremony on the university grounds on that first Wednesday night. I think we had five or six full cars of friends and family who came from the Carmel/Westfield area. It was freezing cold that night, but we managed to keep a large circle of candles going for over an hour. Father Kevin came and said a prayer and the vice president of student affairs shared thoughts from the University. There were over a hundred students there also.

I am the light of the world; whoever follows me will never walk in darkness, but will have the light of life.
                                                              John 8:12

Karl was a very quiet person most of the time. Before he left for school, I remember telling him, "Just remember the golden rule: Be kind to others and they will be kind to you."

He was a B/C student in high school and college, but I do remember one time he got straight A's in middle school. His group of friends was small and tight. He played intramural basketball through high school, and was a great shot blocker with his long arms and 6'4" frame.

His passion, though, was card games. From Star Wars and Magic in his younger years, to poker later on, he loved games and was very good with numbers. When Karl was six, we went to my brother David's wedding in South Carolina. While we were passing time at the lodge, we played a card game called Gin 13. Among a table full of competitive 20- to 50-year-old men, Karl sat down to play a few hands, and ended up beating them all. "Who's the kid? Where did this kid come from? How did he do it?" were some of the questions asked by the men unfamiliar with Karl's card-shark ways. He loved playing card games and anything that involved strategy or analytical thinking.

In fifth grade, Karl qualified and was invited to participate in the "Big M Summer Math Program" at Ball State University for two weeks. This was a program for children gifted in math. We were SO honored and proud to be Karl's family. He was quite the numbers guy! That was the year Livia bought a new Mercury Cougar, and we all piled in to take Karl to Muncie. Ironically, that was the same car we later gave to Karl, and that he drove for three to four years— and the same car he was driving the night he was murdered. I can remember telling Karl to be careful driving in Muncie, and to not be too shy to offer rides to students who weren't fortunate enough to have a car at school. I often have feelings of guilt when I remember some of the advice I gave Karl, before he left for his college years. I know these are only feelings. How could a father really be guilty of teaching his son to be kind to others?

Mother Sharon Mary, who taught with Livia at SMG, came and was very helpful with organizing the funeral mass. Just going to the mortuary was something Livia and I had never done. All our parents were still living, so we had never had to make funeral arrangements or pick out caskets. The support and prayers from the St. Maria Goretti community were overwhelming and much appreciated. The parish hall was full and overflowing for the funeral mass. I remember Fr. Kevin's homily, and how he kept repeating, *"Karl did the right thing."* In a me-me world Karl thought of others first ... and I couldn't be prouder of him.

At the burial service there was a man who brought four white doves. Three were released representing the Trinity, and Livia was given the other one to release representing Karl. They all met in the sky and flew off together. It was an inspiring moment. After the burial service there was a beautiful large luncheon in the parish gym, attended by many. We owe much gratitude to many at St. Maria Goretti Parish.

> *God is our refuge and our strength, an ever-present help in distress. Thus we do not fear, though earth be shaken and mountains quake to the depths of the sea.*
>
> *Psalms 46:2, 3*

After the funeral, we weren't sure what to do with our lives. I took another week off, and then went back to work. I'm sure I was *not* Mr. Productivity for quite a while. Thoughts of Karl were there 24/7, as they still are today.

A friend of ours introduced us to Brooke's Place. Brooke's Place is a local grieving support group, and we attended sessions at Butler University. We were put in a group of other parents who had lost children. We learned a lot from Brooke's Place, but went for only a few months. The one thing that sticks out in my mind about Brooke's Place was a handout they gave us. It showed the many feelings and emotions you go through when grieving. The part I liked was that, instead of some made-up order, the emotions were scrambled all over the page. This was to show that nobody grieves the same as anyone else, and that there is no specific order in which these emotions hit you. Each person is different, and each day is different. I still play in the Brooke's Place Golf Outing every year with my friend, Dan.

On May 13, 2004, the Delaware County Prosecutor's Office told us that they were dropping the murder charges against the 14-year-old suspect. They were charging him in the juvenile courts with the theft of several purses from vehicles parked outside the house where the party was, and where Karl had driven the suspects home from. That was the first time I had heard the suspects had also been stealing from cars during the party. I thought this really showed the suspects' motive for the evening. They weren't there to party and socialize, as Karl and his friends had thought; the suspects were there to get (steal) anything they could get their hands on. The prosecutors also said they believed the juvenile had the murder weapon in his hand before he gave it to the 22-year-old suspect, but that they were waiting for more evidence to come out in the other two trials, and planned to bring the charges back against the 14-year-old when they evaluated that new evidence. We had no choice or part of this decision.

On August 5, 2004, the prosecutors chose to pursue life without parole instead of the death penalty against the 22-year-old. I told the prosecutor, "I do not want to be responsible for the death of any man, but think he might later plead to a lesser offense with this decision." Prosecutor Reed looked me straight in the eye and said, "That will never happen." We were asked to come and talk to the prosecutors before this went public, but we had no choice in this matter either.

In September, 2004, I attended a men's retreat at my Catholic Parish. Many people had asked me, since Karl's death, if I had lost my faith in God, and how God could let this happen to Karl. Actually, with me, I now felt like I needed my faith in God more than ever. I can't imagine how I could have made it through these last four years without that faith. Many times that first year, I felt that God was literally holding me up with his loving hands. The retreat was just what I needed to fire me up. I met a great group of twenty guys and I still see most of them at church every week.

Then, in October, 2004, I was invited to go to a morning coffee group by a friend of mine, Mike Laird. Mike and I play golf together at a local club in Noblesville. That year, 2004, I was president of our men's club, and Mike was secretary. Mike's son, Jake, was an Indianapolis Police Department police officer shot down in the line of duty in August, 2004. So Mike and I had a lot in common. I went to my first Tuesday morning dads meeting, but told Mike that I was doing this just one time, and, "don't expect me to become a regular." I don't think I missed a meeting after that for a couple of years. When I joined the group, there were about eight guys in our group. I think we are up to eighteen now, and each story is different and tragic in its own way.

On January 31, 2005, the 22-year-old suspect pled guilty to armed robbery and murder. The prospective jurors were all waiting outside the courtroom for what was supposed to be the first day of a jury trial. It was no surprise to me that he would plead guilty to avoid a trial, and life without parole, but why did he and his lawyer have to wait until the last minute?

The 22-year-old shooter (I guess I can now call him the 22-year-old murderer), was sentenced in Muncie on March 4, 2005—three days before the anniversary of Karl's murder.

There were probably twenty of our family members there. There were also four of my friends from the Tuesday morning Dads Group in attendance, and one of my Catholic retreat friends. I am forever grateful for the support of my family and friends. Livia and I both were given the opportunity to give impact statements to the judge and audience. The judge sentenced the 22-year-old, that day, to eighty-five years for those crimes against Karl. The judge said his criminal record was the worst she had ever seen. Ten more years was added to that eighty-five-year sentence, when he pled guilty in Marion County court for the crimes he had committed in July of 2003. These were the crimes that he should have been in jail for, long before the time of Karl's murder. He will be eligible for release on March 17, 2079.

On May 10, 2005, the 18-year-old suspect pled guilty to armed robbery resulting in serious bodily harm, and on June 24, 2005, was sentenced to fifty years. The 18-year-old suspect was the one of the three who had the gun when they began the robbery. He will be eligible for release from jail on September 4, 2028. Once again Livia, Brian, and I were joined by many family members and several of my friends from the Tuesday Dads Group.

The next week, I called the prosecutors' office to find out if a date had been set for the third suspect's trial. I did not receive any reply, and began a long process of trying to find out what the status of the third suspect was. Finally on January 3, 2006, I received a call from the prosecutors' office. The prosecutor said, "The juvenile suspect was released sometime after only one year in juvenile detention, and never charged for crimes against Karl." The prosecutors' story, at this point, was that the juvenile was running away from the scene as the murder was taking place. I asked why we were never informed about the juvenile being released from detention. I was told, and this one really gets my blood boiling, "Because the juvenile was never charged with crimes against Karl, you and your family were not considered victims, and did not need to be notified." I wonder about a system that can charge a person with murder and then let him go free. I asked the prosecutors if we would be allowed to see or hear any of the evidence they had collected on this case. I really just wanted to hear what the suspects had to say for themselves during interrogations. We were told no, because it was still an open case. They called it an open case because there is no statute of limitations for murder, and theoretically this suspect could still be charged at a later date. Two out of three suspects ended up with jail sentences. The prosecutors seemed to get to that point and then just called it finished, without completing the job. I was completely baffled. Through the help of my many faithful friends, I have come to believe that God will make the final judgment on these men.

> *Beloved, do not look for revenge but leave room for the wrath; for it is written, "Vengeance is mine, I will repay, says the Lord."*
>
> *Romans 12:19*

Livia and I have started a memorial scholarship in Karl's name. It is the Karl Harford Good Samaritan Scholarship Fund. The "Good Samaritan" title came from a very nice article written in the *Indianapolis Star* a few days after Karl's death. There were some disturbing articles, and some good ones, and this writer, Ruth Holladay, seemed to be the one we liked best. The first recipient was announced in the spring of 2005. Through 2008 we have given over $30,000 in scholarships to seven Good Samaritan students. The recipients are Ball State business students entering their junior or senior year. We have an annual Karl Harford Golf Outing every year to celebrate Karl's life and raise funds for the scholarship fund. The Golf Outing has over 180 golfers, including my golf buddies, parents of Livia's students, Ball State faculty and alumni, and many friends. We are thankful to the many sponsors and golfers who have made this scholarship more than we ever thought it could become.

The emotional roller coaster I have been on in the last four years is unbelievable. I, like many parents, always worried about our young adult children. Mostly, I worried about car wrecks, wild parties, and general safety. Never in my wildest dreams would I have thought one of my sons would have been murdered. Now my son Brian visits his brother and best friend Karl at the cemetery instead of across campus. Livia has returned to teaching at St. Maria Goretti. She says staying busy keeps her from continuous grieving. Karl remains in all our thoughts 24 hours a day. This is a new life for us, and I pray we are adjusting well.

Adjusting, learning to cope, trying to hide, managing.... These are all some of the ways we get through the days. The Tuesday Dads Group has taught me a lot. I like the way Steve put it one day: It's like going through life with a handicap. You carry this handicap, (baggage), whatever, around with you and try to get through each day with as few people noticing as possible. Sometimes you think no one notices, but you are probably wrong. What do you say when you meet someone new, and the conversation turns to family? That person always ends up asking you, "Do you have any children?" I still cringe at this question whenever I hear it. I would never leave Karl out of my family, but is it right for me to tell this person about Karl's tragic life? Will I ruin their day? I doubt it. I usually say I have two sons, Karl and Brian. That's when I continue on by bragging up Brian and hope the conversation moves on to a new subject. If they bring it up again, I'm sorry, they get the full answer.

On Tuesday mornings we also talk about how our lives are changed forever. The lives we all had before were a blessing, and we are thankful for all those times. Now there is a feeling of incompleteness. There is a void that cannot be filled. You will never be the same person you were before. I don't mean to say that every moment of every day is consumed with sadness, but the good times are not, and never will be, what they once were. That upper level of happiness is just not a part of our lives anymore. It is a great blessing to be able to meet once a week with others who you know have similar feelings. Many times at meetings the conversation turns to sports and other enjoyable moments. We all still share a laugh. For me, Tuesday morning is probably the easiest time to cut loose and have a good laugh. We all support each other whenever needed.

I can tell you in the last year I have gone through cancer surgery and my mother died. I had much support from all the men in our group through a very tough year. As tough a year as it was, it is nowhere near as tough as losing a child. As parents we focus our lives on our children. We try to give them the best of everything. We teach, guide, and coach them to grow up to become good citizens. They are the love of our lives. To have another human (??) decide that your son deserves to be executed, is more than just painful. See, there I go again. That is why I need this Tuesday morning Dads Group. So I don't completely lose control.

Several of the dads have mentioned how they enjoy spending time with their lost child at the cemetery. They can sit and talk, and it comforts them to share a conversation with them again. I, on the other hand, have trouble going to the cemetery. It just seems to bring my anger back to the surface. What is good to know from this, is that we are all different. We all are going to grieve differently, and that's okay. There are no rules in this process.

Because of the horrific violence that Karl went through, my wife and I were not able to watch violent movies for a long time (at least that first year). I think that I have adjusted to this better than Livia, but still, we both try to avoid the movies with guns and violence. It is amazing when you do this. You start to wonder if the movie producers know how to make a movie without guns and violence. There just aren't very many movies left to choose from, unless you want to watch a children's cartoon movie.

Then there are those special family celebrations that are lost forever. Karl and Brian were so close. There is no doubt in my mind that they each would have picked the other to be the best man at their wedding. We have been to a few weddings for some of our friends' children. The last one we went to, I remember Livia and I had to make a quick exit in the middle of the Daddy-Daughter dance, because it was just too joyous for us to watch. I hope we didn't offend anyone, but I think they didn't really understand why we were leaving. We probably told them we had somewhere else to go.

We, as dads, try to get together socially a couple of times a year. Mark, Adolf and Marv seem to be our social directors. It is especially important that all our wives are invited to these social events. Men and women don't grieve the same, and this is always a chance for the women to get together to support each other, too. The wives do meet on occasion, but not on a regular basis. As men we continually worry about how our spouses are adjusting, but understand that their emotions and feelings are different than ours.

If you are reading this book because you have lost a son or daughter, I pray that you are learning to cope with your new life. Don't worry about those feelings of, "Why me?"

"Whose fault was this?" or, "Why do I feel so guilty?" Those are normal feelings. I can tell you from my own experience that having a strong faith, and finding others with a similar loss, is helpful. It could be anything from a single person to a large group. Each person has a different story, and each person's story is unique. You will be able to learn and grow from one another and coping will come easier. Understanding and sharing your own individual feelings, your story, and your life will help you find that new person you have become.

Tom Harford

Michael Edward Toomer

MAY 13, 1980 – JULY 21, 1999

"HOW MANY CHILDREN DO YOU HAVE?"

In late July of 1999, my son Christopher, wife Linda and I were having a late breakfast at the Three Sisters Café & Bakery in Broad Ripple, a near north suburb of Indianapolis. Three Sisters is a popular but quiet café, tucked away on a side street. The porch of the converted Victorian house sits next to a nicely busy sidewalk among unique shops and a historic canal. A man at a nearby table said hello and struck up a conversation. He asked if we were a family and if Chris was our son. We responded, "Yes." Then the follow-up question came: "How many children do you have?" I paused, and said, "Two."

That was my first experience, of many that would follow over the next nine years, in which I've responded that I have two sons. "Have" is a present tense verb. I *have* two sons. But one is not physically here with us right now.

That simple question required a quick and powerful reflection as to how I see myself as a father. Michael had just passed away the week before, and the emotional roller coaster of losing a child had just begun.

Michael was with us for nineteen years. A blond-haired, bright-eyed child, he was born on May 13, 1980. He shares that birthday with his older brother, Chris, who was born in 1976. He fulfilled our hope for two children and a somewhat idyllic, middle class lifestyle. His refreshing innocence and energy were a delight and brought tremendous joy to our family and our home.

When Michael was in preschool, we were alerted by a caring teacher to the fact that he was developmentally a bit behind other kids of his age, and that it might be good to have him start kindergarten a year later than anticipated. That was okay. We were happy to give him every maturity advantage that made sense, and to provide him with every opportunity to be successful in his own way.

At the same time, we began to notice that he did have some challenges interacting with other children. It was challenging for him to be a "rough and tumble" kid socially and physically with his peers ... and he seemed, at times, to be a bit out of touch with what was going on around him. Was he just not listening and absorbing what was around him at times? Did he have a hearing problem? A learning disability?

As he progressed through elementary school, Michael's attention to detail was extraordinary: He would get lost for hours in intricate toys or games. His intelligence test scores were near the top of the chart. His social skills were just a bit awkward and less mature than his peers. A major challenge was the time it took him to do simple homework. What was perhaps a fifteen-minute assignment for other kids, might take him hours to complete. He reported that he was always last in the lunch line and did not have enough time to eat or, sometimes, to go outside for recess.

During this time, the effort and energy he expended emotionally and mentally in school to be successful began to take its toll. Eventually, there were occasional tears, headaches and a desire to stay in bed and not go to school.

This situation and challenge was new to us. How do we deal with this? How could we best help Michael make his way through school and live successfully in the world? He was trying very hard to fit in with others, but it was clear that he would need some special support. However, it was unclear for many years as to what type of support was really needed and who could best provide it.

Multiple assessments later, along with a seemingly unending series of teacher conferences and special school accommodations, we received a diagnosis in 1995 that seemed to hit the mark and make some sense to us.

Asperger's Syndrome, still a relatively new diagnosis at that time, includes children and adolescents who are characterized as being of normal or above normal intelligence, who are often focused on narrow areas of interest, and who have some difficulty dealing with social interaction, responding to non-verbal cues, and attaining optimum physical coordination. It is sometimes described as being on a continuum of mild autism.

So what did this mean for Michael as a young adolescent, and for us as parents? As it is said, "diagnoses are interesting and sometimes useful," but the real question for us was how to help Michael live a happy and successful life … how to help him define himself as a happy emerging adult. This was new and unexpected territory for us as parents, and was a daunting task to say the least. But we dug in and were absolutely determined to help him live a happy life, whatever it took … literally, whatever it took in terms of time and resources.

Special tutors and special education support were provided via the school. Computer assisted learning was set up. Counseling support and medication were sought. But it was clear by his freshman year in a new high school that he was drifting, even spiraling, downward and that moderate learning and social concerns were evolving into severe depression, occasional isolation, anxiety, physical tics, and some signs of thought disorder.

We looked for the best schools regionally and nationally that could accommodate a combination of learning and social challenges, and that would meet Michael's needs. We located a school in Utah that we thought would be fine. It appeared to have excellent structure, support and a caring environment.

It did not. He wanted to leave.

After two days in residence he jumped off the roof of his housing unit and badly broke his arm. It was clear that he was feeling desperate.

We brought Michael home and renewed our search for the best place for him to attend school and to get treatment. The next few weeks were chaotic and anxious times as we searched for a place where Michael would be safe and could get back on his feet.

We identified Devereux in Philadelphia. Devereux is a residential setting in which kids and adolescents receive support in all areas of their lives: emotional, social, medical, academic.

The decision to have Michael attend another school and treatment program was difficult for all of us, especially after the crisis in Utah. We were living in Indianapolis and our son was in Philadelphia—more than an eleven-hour drive. We became much more familiar with the Pennsylvania Turnpike than we wanted to be as we made regular trips to visit him. He wanted to be home with us, and we wanted him to be home with us, but we simply could not find the appropriate resources locally to support him adequately at that time.

We were grateful that Devereux was a place, and space, where Michael was able to regain his balance. Nevertheless, after an emotional and challenging eight months there, he returned home to Indianapolis. He was a more confident, less depressed, and much more interactive young man. He had made significant progress in school, as well as with his emotional challenges, but was very happy to be back in our home, in his own room.

With guidance from Devereux, we sought counseling and medical support locally, and located a private school that Michael would attend starting that fall.

The school, Midwest Academy, is located on the north side of Indianapolis (total enrollment of about seventy-five students), and focuses on kids with special needs. It proved to be a good fit for Mike. This was an excellent alternative to the special education programs of larger public or private schools in which he had previously been lost, and where he had been lumped in with kids with disruptive behavior problems.

At Midwest Academy he worked successfully at his own pace, in very small classes, and with the support of

to many teachers and staff who were part of his, and our,
lives during that time.

In 1999, he graduated from high school! Hooray!

We celebrated his success and the friendships that he had
made there ... and talked with Mike about what was next for him.

Linda was so exceptionally supportive of and positive
with Michael during this time, and during the previous
many years. I cannot say enough about her sensitivity, caring
and commitment to him. As a wonderful mother, she was
willing to do whatever it took to make his years following
high school happy and successful. This sensitivity was clearly
part of Michael's personality as well. His caring and feelings for other people were immense. This extended to the
"fifth family member" as well: our dog, Muffy, was a soft,
white Bichon that Michael took care of with all his heart and
soul. They bonded from the get-go and the image of Muffy
nuzzled up against Michael's chest as they went to sleep at
night is so special to us.

Mike was very bright and understood this. Perhaps this was
a burden in some ways, as he set very high expectations for
himself in terms of achievement. I don't know. He was a
spelling champ in elementary school. His memory for facts
and events was excellent. We successfully worked the cross-
words in the paper a couple of times each week, and I worked
hard to keep up with his growing vocabulary and to do my
part in completing the crossword puzzles! His SAT scores
were extremely high (he took the un-timed version). His
desire to go to college was strong, it seemed, and yet his
anxiety about leaving home and succeeding in college still
seemed to be severe.

104

As he completed high school, we mutually settled on a plan for him to live with us at home and start part-time classes at a local university in a technical program that interested him. Our hope was that over the next few years he could successfully complete a degree program of some type and start to live independently, perhaps in a housing situation with some daily supervision and support.

That summer, however, he became more depressed and less enthused about going to college. He also felt the pressure of wanting to work part-time, but needed the special assistance and support of a job coach in order to do so.

What to do? The summer was not going very well.

At that time I seriously considered quitting work and simply going to live with Mike somewhere ... somewhere he could be happy and have no pressure or expectations at all. Would he be happy living in a rural area and working as a family on a small farm? Could he live in a group home for young adults with daily support? Should I just move with him "to the beach" and hang out? Again, more questions than answers! How could we best help him?

We did not have time to take the next step, whatever that might have turned out to be. He made his decision to resolve his anxieties and to leave.

It was early in the day.

I recall exactly where I was, with whom I was sitting, the subject of our conversation, the anxious interruption that indicated that I had an urgent phone call. Linda never called me at work unless it was urgent. This was urgent. Michael would not wake up. He was in bed and unresponsive. She knew he was dead. He had taken an overdose of prescription medication.

The roller coaster of emotions and the blur of activity began.

In some regards, it has not stopped since that day.

Michael left two messages for us that we are aware of. Did we miss others?

One was related to music.

Red House Painters was one of his favorite bands at that time.

The CD *Down Colorful Hill* was cued to the song, "Michael," and set to repeat.

> *Michael, where are you now?*
> *Michael, where are you now?*
>
> *...Do you remember our first subway ride?*
> *...I remember your warm smile in the sun.*
> *...My best friend.*

What was going through his mind? How could we have helped that night? Did we miss a cry for help?

Another message was on the computer—Michael had changed the screen-saver on our family computer the night he died.

It read: *"Death is inevitable; resistance is futile."*

This is a quote from *Star Trek* and refers to "the Borg."

The Borg are an android race who are connected mentally and emotionally by a "common force." Their fate is inextricably tied to one another and they cannot resist the force or separate themselves from it. *Star Trek* was one of Michael's favorite TV programs, one that we often watched together. He followed the characters in this program deeply, not just casually.

Did Michael feel that resistance was futile? That life was futile?

Was this message his way of spiritually telling us that it was okay ... and that it was his way of moving on to a place where he is ultimately connected to others?

Was this Michael's way of telling us that death is inevitable for all of us ... and that we must make our way through this world until that time comes?

Michael was very philosophical and often looked for deeper meaning in what he experienced and read. I assume that there may be connections in the messages he left that we do not fully understand. And, did we miss other messages?

I was his father. I had not kept him safe. I had failed.

I was so numb the first year after Michael's passing that I really did not feel or absorb how my life had changed. I was so focused on just getting through the next hour, or day, or week ... or supporting Linda ... or sleeping through a night without horrible dreams, that it was just a blur.

The second year was more difficult than the first.

Hard to believe. But true.

Without my co-workers encouraging me to make it through each day of the first two years following Michael's passing, I would simply not have made it. They helped provide me with a continuing purpose to put one foot in front of the other, sometimes with great difficulty. They helped remind me that there was value in my life beyond a feeling of profound grief, guilt and despair ... and most of the time they didn't even know they were doing this. I could name them, but the list would go on and on.

There were times during meetings at work when I simply would mentally check out for a few minutes. My mind would wander. I would need to take bathroom breaks to avoid tears in the middle of a discussion. People understood. Michael was *always* in my thoughts. It seemed that I could, in fact, hold two thoughts in my mind at the same time: what I was working on, and vivid memories of Michael.

People encouraged me to keep working; to keep adding value to others' lives at work; and to do what was right for my family. This helped me to resist a downward self-indulgent spiral and to not let myself be *pulled* further down, either. To John and Charlie, "J" and many, many others, I am very grateful. More than they know.

It would have been good to be part of the Dads Group during that time, but alas, I did not join the group until about "year five" after Michael had passed away. It was mentioned to me by our pastor that I "had to meet" another dad who had lost a child. That dad was Adolf Hansen. From Adolf, I learned that a dads group had been formed and that I was welcome to stop by on Tuesday mornings for coffee at a local hotel restaurant. So, I checked it out and it has now become an important part of my life and my routine.

Early on Tuesday morning we can be debating a Buckeye, Bulldog, Hoosier or Boilermaker game and insulting each other's favorite team, and the next minute we can be discussing one dad's inability to sleep the night before ... or his fear of losing another child ... or the loss of a parent.

The group works that way, moving naturally from one topic to another with no agenda, and no "forcing" of dads to talk about anything they don't want to talk about. It is coffee, a bite to eat, and a deep connection with other dads that is difficult to adequately describe, but that is profoundly meaningful.

Without fail, I feel understood and supported each time I am with this group. I may not feel "better" or "good," in part because our discussions often dig deep and stir old feelings and emotions about losing Michael; but I am always grateful for others who naturally understand my emotion, my thoughts, my roller coaster ride.

A conclusion I have reached while in the Dads Group is that *nothing can happen to me that can be worse than losing a child* (nothing, that is, other than losing another child, which I resist thinking about).

To quote a dad, "Tragedy can sometimes be strangely liberating."

In a loss as powerful and compelling as the loss of a child, comes a strange feeling of resilience and increased freedom to take risks. "Bring it on world! I can take anything you can throw at me because I have experienced the worst thing that I can imagine. And I have survived."

I don't consider this feeling of resilience to be arrogant, or a blind avoidance of life's sometimes harsh realities, but rather a profound understanding that I am still putting one foot in front of the other; that I am clearer about what is truly important to me; that in my life, I have less patience for the trivial and more respect for the high-value-adding aspects of day-to-day living; that in my work, I have more sensitivity and understanding to many who are working hard to make a difference, while I also have less patience for those who seek control for control's sake or who "play games" with others (there is little time for waste or for ego). So, to those with whom I have sometimes been unusually candid or blunt, I offer a blanket apology, eh?

It is too easy to get caught up in the trivial stuff in life, and the dads understand this. And even though our Tuesday morning conversations may address a football game, or politics, or golf, there exists a feeling of mutual support and common understanding that provides a bond ... and breathes the hope that we will make it through another week.

And if I were to write this narrative at a different time in my life, at a different place in my grief process, I would likely talk about different aspects of grief, or talk about the experience differently.

For those who expect grief to subside with time, I can only say, "Yes, it will" ... followed by a quick, "Or perhaps, it won't."

Grief will visit whenever it wishes.

And, life is not filled with constant despair and regret. There are memories of great times that flash through my mind, and I have dreams about Michael that are intensely real and positive: hiking; swimming; family birthdays; favorite songs.

I dream a lot and dreams are a gift to me. Even vivid, sometimes sad, dreams that place Michael and me together again are cherished.

So when grief visits, I consider it a gift, too. The "gift of grief" connects me spiritually and deeply to Michael.

I trust that I will never lose this ability to grieve and, most importantly, to connect with a profound sense of thankfulness that he was with us for nineteen years.

Prior to losing Michael, I didn't read the obituaries, but I do now ... nearly every day. It is a curiosity about other children who have passed away ... and other parents and families who are grieving. There are three basic categories of obituaries in my mind: One, the obituaries of folks who are "older" and are dying of natural causes, e.g., "Harold was 82; send your memorial contributions to the American Cancer Society." Two, mid-life adults who obviously are leaving spouses, younger children, siblings. They may have died suddenly from a traffic accident, early-in-life cancer, or a violent death. And, three, children or young adults.

I usually read the obituaries of children or young adults thoroughly, often projecting my own ideas of what may have happened in a particular situation, and emotionally reaching out in spirit to those parents and siblings who are grieving a loss. Some are infants shortly after birth; some are children who have been chronically ill; some are "sudden deaths." I fill in the blanks and remember Michael. It is a somber regular connection with Michael ... and with others, especially parents, who are experiencing a loss. Some days there are no children or young adults in the Indianapolis obituaries. That's a good day. That's a day in which everyone noted in the obituaries lived long lives and passed away "in the right order." Our children are not supposed to precede us in death.

Another regular connection that I maintain with Michael is to wear something of his nearly every day. During the first two to three years after he passed away, I was obsessive about this. I wore a T-shirt or socks, his ring, perhaps a pendant around my neck, or kept in my pocket a shell or rock that we had collected on a beach or a hike. I fiddled with these articles incessantly in a rhythm of connection with Michael that was, and continues to be, very reassuring. I still wear his ring every day and, after nine years, I observe that the T-shirts are getting a bit more frayed and in some cases a bit smaller (or, I'm getting larger). But the shirts wear well and I treasure the feeling of having a part of him close to me as I go about my life.

Linda also had the wonderful idea of sewing many of Michael's favorite T-shirts into a quilt. It hangs in our home and is a constant reminder of who he was and where he/we had traveled.

After nearly ten years, the roller coaster of emotions continues. The highs and lows may be more familiar to me, and somewhat less intense ... but nonetheless, they continue.

Our Dads Group has discussed frequently that we are on a journey ... of life and of grief ... each in our own way and our own time.

Recently, a dad pointed out that it is a journey, yes, but also an odyssey: a journey has a destination and an implied resolution or successful ending, while an odyssey is more like a wandering, with no clear destination or resolution in sight.

My emotional roller coaster is an odyssey of sorts. There is no specific destination or resolution. Life just "is." And that is okay. I am still learning to accept it for what it is, and more importantly, for what it can be. And I am privileged to share this unplanned odyssey with the other dads in our group ... a gathering of fine men in a group that no one wants to join.

As dads who have lost children, we wander ... sometimes together ... sometimes alone. But we each make our way.

How many children do I have?

"I have two sons."

Jerry Toomer

Jennifer Pokorny

OCTOBER 25, 1984 – APRIL 8, 2004

JEN WAS BORN OCTOBER 25, 1984, WITH PRETTY BLUE EYES. SHE made friends easily and was very smart, doing well in school. She always liked to perform in some way, whether it was dancing or singing to a song. I think she would have loved to have been a performer—a singer, dancer, or actress. However, her talent and brilliance were in her creative artistic nature. She combined definite opinions and determination with a smile and a sense of humor, and an ability to make others want to be around her.

I think the following statement from one of Jen's friend's sums her up very well: "I went to grade school and high school with Jenny. We became not only teammates, but good friends. I thought she was a beautiful and intelligent girl who was there for me, on and off the tennis court. I looked up to Jenny. She was confident and sharp with her wit and was always surrounded by friends. She had character, which in high school is hard to find. She had a magnetic, strong personality that got people's attention and gained her respect. There are always those few select people that for whatever reason stand out, they don't blend, they just can't. Jenny was just that special, loved in life and loved forever in memory."

Jen grew into a beautiful young adult and was a Dean's List student at Ball State University, where she focused her attention on landscape architecture. She was a sophomore, and was looked to as a leader within her class. I could not have asked more from a daughter, and her parents were so proud of her. When she came home to visit I always had the feeling when she walked in that, "everything in the world is right and perfect."

For me, my life changed on April, 8, 2004, when the doorbell rang around 5:30 p.m. I had just returned from a business trip to Chicago, and I thought it was a friend I was expecting to stop by. It was a nonuniformed police chaplain. He asked if I was alone and if he could come in. I had no thought that anything bad was about to happen. I even made small talk and a joke about letting someone in that I did not know. He informed me that Jennifer was dead. I don't recall how he worded things exactly, as I was in disbelief. I felt as if life was draining out of me. I know I cried, but not like I still do today (both from good memories and sadness), and I don't know if I really comprehended the loss.

Jen had called me on April 6th to check in, and we talked about things, and all had seemed fine. We had our usual joke and laughter about a recent *Seinfeld* repeat that I was watching. I miss her laugh and sense of humor. I told her that I loved her and would see her at Easter. She spoke to her mom, Kathi, the next day, which was her mom's birthday. It was also Jen's one-year anniversary with her boyfriend, and they had just returned from dinner and were going to meet friends. All seemed fine, Kathi would tell me later.

We don't really know what happened other than she was found by her roommate, and she had taken her life. We were told that she got up on the morning of the 8th, took a test (she received an A), met with her landscape project team, took a shower and had lunch with her boyfriend. There was nothing indicating that anything was wrong or perceived by others to be a worry to her. No note was left behind. The autopsy was negative, indicating that there was nothing in her system that would result in a loss of knowing what she was doing. We have no idea what happened, why, or if it was somehow an accident.

The next day, I went to Muncie to see my baby one last time. I did not know if I could see her in this way, but I forced myself to do it. I am so happy that I did, even in such a difficult situation. My life will never be the same without her in it, but I did feel some comfort that I saw her, talked to her and kissed her forehead one last time. I then attended a memorial service held in her classroom, arranged by one of her professors. So many of her fellow students attended as well.

I spoke at her funeral because it was something I had to do. I had spoken at my father's funeral and had barely gotten through it. For Jen's, I struggled at first, but regained my composure as I looked out to see how many people were there—her friends, her mom's and my friends, as well as others who wanted to be there. At that moment, I told those attending that I would get through this because I wanted them to know who Jen was and what made her so special. I discussed various parts of her life, her successes, her weaknesses, her sense of humor, our relationship and funny things that had happened in her life. I wanted to celebrate her life. Later that night I would receive a message on the answering machine from a friend and business colleague. He said that I had done a wonderful job in letting those who did not know Jen understand who she was. He said it would have an impact on how he would relate to his daughter going forward.

This is a very important and meaningful thing for me, to celebrate Jennifer's life whenever possible. This provides me great comfort. Yes it can cause me to be sad and cry, but there are also tears of joy from so many wonderful memories. I want to continue to celebrate and remember those great moments of her life. I want to remember the most obscure moments that only a parent would know, like the look of relief and joy on her face after her first hit in a softball game. Although she did not have the best physical talent, I still remember this moment for the joy inside I felt for her. The elegance of her look when she played the flute in junior high. The joy and laughter we shared in wrestling for the TV clicker. I want to share these memories and so many more with others who remember as well, and to let them know that it is okay to talk about Jen. It is okay to laugh and cry about Jen. I say all the time, "Jen would have liked that," or, "Jen would have said this." She was, and always will be, so much a part of my life that it is important that others understand that it is okay to remember and share. There is comfort and healing there.

Family and friends do not want to "go there" out of fear that it will make me feel uncomfortable and sad. They just want me to be better. Well, it may make me sad—but it also might make me happy that they would recall some good memory about Jen. Any memory of her is better than no memory of her. The day I put my baby's memories away, is the day I have completely lost her. I have lost her in the physical world. I will not lose her in my thoughts. You cannot be how others would have you be. You need to be the way you are.

I have found comfort in having her pictures around the house, and I continue to watch videos of her from time to time. These are, again, moments of joy and sadness, but mostly they are always so positive. To simply remember those wonderful times. I have found comfort in keeping in touch with her friends periodically. I have gone and done things like attending a Dave Matthews concert, because Jen loved Dave Matthews and going with her friends. It reminds me of her and of other times, like when I took her to see the Teenage Mutant Ninja Turtles, *Phantom of the Opera,* Smashing Pumpkins and Red Hot Chili Peppers.

I talk to Jen all the time. Whether it is looking at a picture of her or just out loud. I talk to her and let her know that I am thinking about her. I have a certain hand gesture I make as I walk by a picture of her making the same gesture. When we used to travel in the car listening to songs—we had many similar musical tastes, lucky for me—I would hold out my hand, and she would place her hand in it briefly, almost like giving someone "five." And still today, if I happen to hear a song I know she liked, I will at times hold out my hand as if she is there, and somehow imagine the slight feel of the weight of her hand there. Comfort, memory and joy.

I have kept in touch with some of her friends, but only if they are receptive to it. In nearly all cases they have contacted me to let me know they still think about Jen. Recently, her roommate contacted me and we had a wonderful time talking about Jen and what she meant to us both. Some friends have fallen by the wayside, which is expected as time goes by and their lives continue to grow.

I joined the Dads Group in 2005, approximately one year after Jen passed away. I was reluctant at first, as I did not have a great experience with the counselor I had seen immediately following Jen's passing. The counselor had no impact on me, as she merely stated that my feelings were normal and valid. After three visits I sent her on her way. You see, she could not comprehend my loss unless she had experienced the same thing. The Dads Group is made up of fathers who have had the same unfortunate experience. This is not a group you want to join; however, this is a group that can provide much understanding and empathy. The group meets every Tuesday morning at 7 a.m. in a coffee shop at a hotel. Some attend most every meeting, and some attend, as I do, when they feel they need it.

Our group has sadly grown from nine at the time I joined, to sixteen now. They are all a great group of guys, and many I have things in common with such as golf, work, etc. This group is a place where I can share my feelings and express my pain and loss. We all share our feelings and how we cope with them, and see that these feelings and thoughts are normal and expected. This is one of the few places where I will cry in public. The simple fact is that they "get it." They understand what I am feeling. They know that this feeling I have will always be there and that it is alright to feel the things I do. No other outlet provides this much caring and understanding.

One of the fathers, Jerry Baker, had one of those rubber wrist bands created for his son that says "Never Forgotten," and he shared them with the group. I wear mine every day. It is not the point that I could ever forget, it is the point that

Jennifer is always there with me. I get asked about it all the time, as these types of bands are very prevalent and stand for so many causes. It does force a difficult discussion that most people are unaware of, but it is not something I will hide. It is a normal thing when you meet new people as friends, or for business, to ask, "Do you have any children?" The answer is always yes. I have two. At that point I determine the level of knowledge they need to have. The most important thing is that I have two children. I will never ignore or deny Jennifer. She is always with me in my heart and mind.

The Dads Group allows me to share with others who understand. If you are able to find a similar group, whether it is all fathers, or mothers and fathers, be sure that all feelings and thoughts can be shared with those who understand. If there are some in the group who cannot, that is okay, as hopefully they will learn to share over time. The key is that the group allows for sharing, understanding, pain, anger, sadness, tears and laughter. There will always be some anger and disappointment with family and friends who do not understand and who simply want your life to be better and for you to forget the pain. Don't ever let your child and your memories fade away. You are always one memory away from sadness, but how you deal with it is a frame of mind. A group like our Dads Group will help in so many ways.

There will always be sadness, but I am so lucky to be Jennifer's father and to have the feelings of joy she still brings to me today.

Anthony Pokorny

Jonathan "JR" Pavey

FEBRUARY 10, 1966 – MARCH 14, 2005

THE DATE WAS MARCH 14, 2005, WHEN WE RECEIVED THE PHONE call every parent fears. It was early on a Monday morning. My wife, Jacquie, took the call. Her scream, her expression, told me the news was bad—and I was certain it was JR. He had been found dead, in his home, by his wife's cousin. When someone has an addiction, you jump every time the phone rings—especially late at night or early in the morning. You fear "the call." You hope it never comes, but you are not shocked when it does. You almost have a sense that you "knew" somehow.

I think about my son JR all the time. He was our first-born, the first grandchild on my wife's side, and the first male Pavey grandchild on mine. His birth was uneventful and exciting—we were ready to be good parents. Yet, when someone suggested I tell his/our story, when I tried to put down my thoughts, I realized the task was unbelievably hard, overwhelming even. When you lose someone you love, especially a child, you are bombarded with so many emotions that it is hard to breathe, to think, to comprehend. Later, when reality has set in, you are assailed with the "what ifs," the "if onlys," the "why didn't I sees...." If I had to analyze my reasons for doing this, I guess I would say I want you to know my son—and maybe by telling you about him, I can understand what really happened.

JR was a bright and inquisitive little boy—full of energy and curiosity. "A real keeper," my wife often said. While I was busy starting a career, Jacquie stayed home—and we both nurtured and spent time with our son. We read all the books, were determined to do things right, and JR was the focus of our life. Like all parents, we wanted our son to be happy, and wanted to protect him from life's disappointments and struggles; but we knew his life wouldn't, and couldn't, be perfect, so we also tried to prepare him to handle the inevitable adversities that would come his way. Now, looking back, somehow this lesson didn't take!

JR was a great kid. We did all the normal things—early on, there were family outings, cousins galore, walks, bike rides, library visits and book reading! As a small child, he would listen to stories for hours. Some, like The Poky Little Puppy, he knew by heart and knew when to turn the page. After his brother Jeff arrived, when JR was just over three, we felt our family was complete and the normal activities continued. Soon nursery school, Sunday school, sporting activities, family vacations, and Indian Guides were added to the mix. We were busy and happy and involved as a family.

As JR grew, I realized he was different from me. I loved sports—both as a participant and as a spectator. Although JR loved playing hockey, he really preferred more solitary activities. I was okay with that—even though I couldn't help much as he tinkered and experimented and created in our garage. There was always something going on out there—and rarely was there room for a car! A client of mine, whose kids raced go karts, gave me an old kart—not working of course—and JR wouldn't rest until he had an operating vehicle. He started collecting old worn out mowers from the neighbors, and worked ceaselessly until he had a functional mower and engine for the go kart. I think it was five years after he had graduated from college, that we finally got rid of the last of the engine parts. He didn't confine himself to small engines though. Once he made a wind wagon—a sailboat on wheels—from parts of an old sailboat. He had enjoyed such a device on the beach in Hilton Head—and brought the idea home. He terrorized the neighbors on Pleasant View Drive as he "sailed" down the street!

I recall that, when he was twelve, to my great horror, he took his brand new ten-speed bicycle apart. There it was, strewn all over the garage floor—and I had no idea how to reassemble it. Fortunately, he did! His fifth grade teacher had taught a small group how to work on their bikes. He reassembled his ten-speed—with one small spring left over. When I asked him why he had done that, his calm response was, "How else would I know how it worked?"

I remember the summer he discovered sailing. He was introduced to it at summer camp, and we bought a used Snark, a Styrofoam dinghy really, to see if his interest was genuine. He and his one best friend, M, literally wore it out that first summer. At camp the following summer, instead of choosing many activities, he chose sailing for seven out of the ten free periods. He always was a bit obsessive! We were able to join the sailing club at Geist. JR took lessons and raced, both alone and with friends. By this time we were aware he really wasn't motivated by competition against others, but more by competition with himself. Sailing met that need and he loved it: JR against the water and the wind. He had a Laser, encouraged us to purchase a Thistle, and really hit his stride one year when we visited Jacquie's family in Cape Cod. He rigged up an apparatus that had the Thistle on the bottom, a windsurfer inside, and the Laser upside down on top of it all. What a picture we made, pulling all of this behind our little LeBaron all the way to Cape Cod. I still remember him vanishing from sight as he flew down the Atlantic coast on his windsurfer. He was in his element.

JR did have a dark side, which could appear suddenly. Starting around age seven or eight, he would sometimes become moody, sullen, withdrawn. I'm not sure why I recall certain incidents now—perhaps in retrospect they seem like warnings. At the time, I attributed them to a little boy growing up. When he was eight or nine, he threw a rock at a passing motorist, damaging her car. We, of course, paid for the damage and calmly required JR to walk up to the lady's door and apologize for his behavior. She was gracious and complimented him for speaking up and taking responsibility. When we tried to get the reason for the action to begin with, we were met with stony silence—and the issue was never resolved to our satisfaction.

When he was ten, he played in the Squirt Division of the Indianapolis Hockey Association. That year, his team was very good and won the championship. JR was a very good skater and always played on the first or strongest line. He wasn't the star, but he certainly contributed significantly to the team's success. He had improved so much that he received special praise from his coach. At the year-end party, I noticed he was keeping to himself and not joining in. His comment when I asked why: "I wasn't important to the team."

This shyness and antisocial behavior continued, and try as I might, I couldn't get to its root. He excelled in school, but he never wanted to be singled out. He wouldn't join school activities and, even when his mom threatened, he refused to go to a prom. On the night of his senior prom, I noticed our neighbor's daughter all dressed up, leaving for the event. We didn't even know it was happening. And where was JR? In the garage, working on one of his projects.

He had a few friends—but just a few. One special friend, his sailing buddy, M, lived nearby. At some point, in junior high school, he and M started experimenting with more than engines. M had older brothers, and alcohol and marijuana were readily available. I blame naïvety on my part, the fact that the problem was new to our community, our lack of education, and disbelief! Our son, a pothead? Never! We later learned that some children can become hooked from the first joint or the first drink, and looking back, I guess that was JR. We sent him to counseling, we punished him, we limited his contact with friends, we read books and went to meetings— but nothing worked. And, I guess we eventually just turned a blind eye because he continued to excel in school and to play hockey. It couldn't be real, could it? Jacquie recalls him telling her, "Life is so much clearer and brighter after I have had a joint or a drink." Honestly, I don't think we ever really made any progress, but JR became skilled at working the system. Even though his mom perfected the art of sniffing and kissing simultaneously, JR knew how to deceive us. He said all the right things, would lay off when necessary, and then would resume his activities as soon as our guard was down. His younger brother knew, his friends knew, but we kept believing him, and in him. He not only survived high school, but did so in fine fashion. He graduated with honors and off he went to Purdue.

Out of sight, out of mind—except for the weekly phone calls. JR joined a fraternity, he seemed to make new friends, he made good grades, and he was set on his major. What could be wrong with this picture? What was wrong, of course, was that the habits already set in motion were now ingrained. He drank too much, he smoked too much, and he was dependent on chemicals to relax, to interact, and to socialize. Already his problem was unmanageable—but he thought he was in complete control.

His sophomore year he met a spectacular redhead, and he and K dated throughout his time at Purdue. She was a stabilizing force for him, and he planned to marry her. There is no point in detailing his college career any further; suffice it to say, he graduated with honors, had found his true love, found a good job—and moved away.

The job was as a detail rep for a large pharmaceutical company—a big mistake we now know. It was one of those jobs that flew in the face of JR's talents and forced him out of his comfort zone. Fear of rejection and fear of failure had plagued him since childhood, so this was no job for him. He was sent to Wichita, Kansas. Also a mistake. It was far from home, and too small for a big city kid. Nevertheless, he seemed to be succeeding. He made a few friends, worked hard, made excellent presentations, bought a Hobie Cat to sail on a nearby reservoir, and started to work with radio-controlled planes. At this time he still knew how to get the job done. The truth was, however, that the same, now well-established patterns continued behind the scene. Bravado and alcohol got him by. He performed well for a couple of years—but then his employer became aware of the situation. They gave him several chances and finally he quit his job. Also, K, his girlfriend, aware of the addiction problem, visited him once and decided her future was not with him.

JR survived the following several months only because of a young couple who took him in. We think it was a six-month drunk. Many years later, his brother Jeff filled us in on what had happened next: JR had decided to commit suicide. He knew that he would do it, but was still working out the details of where and when. But then someone found him, connected with him, and invited him to church. In my view, the church was odd, almost cultish, but it appealed to JR's psyche. Jeff told us that JR walked out of that church service, still thinking about suicide, when a warm feeling traveled from his head to his feet. He saw the Lord—and he knew he would not end his life. Instead, he picked himself up, found a job as a phlebotomist, and enrolled in Wichita State University to pursue his Med Tech degree.

We, who had been watching this drama from afar, didn't know the details. We had visited him a few times, and he had come home occasionally—but, as before, he kept us in the dark and reacted angrily when we questioned him. We agreed to help him borrow money for school and rejoiced in his decision. Surely his life would be better now! He was back on track! He even toyed with the idea of medical school. We are sure the drinking and drugging continued, but he was in control once again—or so he thought. After obtaining his degree—again with honors—he decided to leave Wichita, and an extensive job search took him to Chicago. He was employed as a technologist by a prominent Chicago hospital and, although he was living in a questionable part of town, he seemed happy. His boss really liked him and even involved him in some teaching—he was a smart, personable young man!

JR reconnected with a branch of the same church he had found in Wichita, and moved from his first job to another. The new job put him in charge of a small reference lab, where he was really the "go-to" person on procedures, computer questions, inspections—everything. There he met L, a lovely Filipino lady whom he was determined to marry.

All during this time, the patterns established so long ago were still playing themselves out. He didn't allow his addictions to interfere with work—but evenings and weekends were a different matter.

Still from afar, we tried to stay in close touch. We called—and sometimes he returned the calls, sometimes not. We visited—with the visits getting mixed reviews. Occasionally, he visited us. When we were together, everyone was on edge. We hid the wine, refrained from partaking ourselves, and tried to keep peace. He was sketchy on the details of his life, but we were aware that his job was stressful and that he certainly was still drinking.

When the lab closed, he joined the takeover company as a sales rep—back to his first disastrous job—and it shortly put him over the edge. By this time he had married L, his true love. They bought their first house and threw themselves into updating and renovating. I recall telling him that it seemed things were as good as they had ever been. He agreed. The picture was completed by the arrival of Tom, an abandoned beagle who, along with L, was his best friend to the end.

Then, in 2001, we received a call that JR had decided to check himself into a prestigious rehab center in Chicago. We breathed a sigh of relief, hoping this truly would give him the support he needed to get his life back on track. We kept encouraging him, supporting him emotionally, not ever giving up. Parents (and probably spouses) of addicts must be the most naïve people in the world. They just keep believing it will get better! And, for more than a year, it did. JR was sober, he lost weight, he found another good job, he attended a Bible study group that he loved, and he even was admitted to Loyola to pursue a master's degree in counseling. He and L went to church, and enjoyed their home and garden. But it was too much. He had stopped concentrating on his recovery and he crashed, he relapsed, he fell off the wagon—whatever you want to say. From today's perspective, that year was the best he and L, and we, had. The next three years were a roller coaster.

A new job led to new problems and, for the first time, JR's drinking wasn't confined to evenings and weekends. It had entered the workplace. Another rehab, another job, another rehab, another job. All through this, L stood by his side, and we blessed her for her strength, and for being there for him. She was our ally, because he wanted little or nothing to do with us—even though we never turned him away. I think he feared we and L would gang up on him. Once, L was desperate and asked for help. Jeff was in graduate school at Indiana University and was between semesters. He agreed to step up. To keep JR sober long enough to get into rehab, the two of them took a road trip to South Carolina to enjoy the sun and the boats. The trip was no joy ride, but it served its purpose, and Jeff didn't have any difficulties with his brother. I breathed a huge sigh of relief when they returned safely! But that rehab and subsequent halfway house didn't accomplish much for all its promise.

Then there was the final rehab, back at Rush, the same hospital that had helped him the first time. A detox session at the hospital had sent him there. The date: November of

2004. JR was thirty-eight years old and had been an addict for half of that time.

This time we were able to attend "Family Week" at Rush Hospital. Family Week is a time when family members—parents, siblings, spouses, and children of those in treatment—attend a several-day workshop with their addicts to gain understanding and to show support. We really warmed to the patients and to their families; we cried with them as they told their stories and we told ours. We were surprised to learn what a leader JR was—how he helped others and gave them hope. Why couldn't they have helped him in return? We had a good visit, though it was marred by one confrontation. He seemed to want to free himself from his addiction; he seemed to know what to do; yet when we offered our support and help, he turned on us yet again. His roommate consoled us by explaining that that was how JR coped: by pushing people who cared about him, away. He was so defensive and fearful! Our love and admiration for his wife grew yet again.

We worried about Christmas. His wife had gone home to the Philippines to visit family, and we didn't want him to be alone. We even called his counselor at Rush. JR really didn't want to come home. For many years he had rejected our Christmas celebration, which was a real sadness for the rest of us. This year his church had a retreat, and he wanted to go. The participants were aware of his problems. Apparently the retreat was a success and all felt renewed. When he returned to Chicago, JR stayed with one of the pastors for a while, but really wanted to go home. His brother Jeff flew in from Seattle to spend some time with him, and left filled with uncertainty. He wasn't sure that JR was committed to his recovery even though he was trying to do the ninety AA meetings in ninety days.

In February I was desperate to help. His mother wanted to go to Chicago for his February 10th birthday. JR didn't want that. I tried repeatedly to arrange to go up to visit him—just the two of us. He had all kinds of excuses why that wouldn't work: he was already working a temporary job, he had friends coming by, etc.

One night he called. It was rare for him to initiate a call. He had been applying for jobs in the Chicago area and even had had some interviews. He really wanted to get away from bench tech jobs—and one company had come through. It appeared to be a dream job, with a very good company. Obviously he had been drinking. When I asked him why, he said, "What if I fail?" I said, "What if you don't?" It was at this point that I finally accepted the fact that JR was convinced he could no longer perform up to his résumé, even sober and clean. He had abused so long that his considerable abilities had been impaired. His fear of failure once again reared its ugly head—and he was afraid his long-suffering wife would finally leave him. He had lost the ability, and maybe the will, to start over.

That last weekend, I wanted to go to Chicago; he asked me not to come. He must have been in hell. He drove drunk, wrecked his wife's beautiful Mustang, got arrested, and on and on. I will regret, until the day I die, not making that trip. We later learned that his friends had tried to reach him, too, because they had had plans together that weekend, but he didn't answer the door or the phone. He probably died sometime on Sunday, but his body wasn't discovered until Monday morning. It wasn't an overdose or a deliberate act. His body just gave out. In desperation my wife said, "I believe God saw his suffering and knew he couldn't recover, so He took him home." I certainly hope that is true. What a sad end for such a promising young man.

When JR died, he left a hole in our hearts that will never be filled. He left so many questions that will never be answered. We met and talked with many people at his funeral in Chicago whose lives he had touched in a positive way. A former co-worker flew in for the service. The couple who had helped him in Wichita drove in. His boyhood friend M and his college friend J were there. Why could he not see himself as others saw him? Why didn't AA help him as it has helped so many others? Why wasn't L's love and our love enough? We asked why our prayers hadn't been answered. But maybe they were.

During the funeral, and for a couple of weeks afterward, there was an outpouring of sympathy and support, but then friends and family went back to their lives, and we were left with our pain, our questions, our emptiness, our grief. Our lives had changed forever. My wife Jacquie, my son Jeff, JR's widow L and I supported each other then and now. We talked about JR, we remembered him, we grieved together. But there were times when we needed to grieve alone—Jacquie as his mother, Jeff as his brother, L as his wife, and I as his father. Jeff lived in Seattle and went back to his life there. Jacquie had friends and family and was able to share with them. L was lonely, but she had her grown sons. I was caught; I could share only with Jacquie—and I needed help!

I believe God saw my need—and of course sent a messenger. An acquaintance said, "I have someone I want you to meet." His name was Mark; he invited me to a breakfast to meet a group of fathers called simply the Dads Group. There were no officers, no one was in charge; there was no agenda, no dues were collected. This was a group of seventeen or eighteen men who shared a tragedy: we had all lost a child. Ever since that first Tuesday breakfast, more than two years ago, I rarely miss. Occasionally I am out of town—but I can tell you that each of us makes Tuesday morning a priority. My weeks are better when I attend.

Each of us has a different story. Our children have perished prematurely. Some were police officers who died in the line of duty; some died as a result of accidents, murders, diseases or addictions. No one judges another, no loss is greater than another. We understand! But the breakfasts aren't sad occasions. We talk, tell stories, laugh, and share life's problems. Sometimes we just sit and feel the bond that joins us. When one of us is having a bad day or week, we are there for him and can truly say, "I've been there!" It is often hard for men to talk about their feelings, their struggles, their grief. In this group, we can talk, one dad to another. Often outsiders mean well, but say stupid and even hurtful things. I can see judgment in their eyes. That never happens in the Dads Group. We can laugh about the stupid comments and share comments we have heard. We can sympathize about friends and family who think we should move on. We draw strength from each other, and we help each other reevaluate and understand what is really important in our lives. We don't try to forget our grief—we really don't want to—we just want to get through the day.

This is an amazing group of men. We genuinely like each other and have become good friends. The group has been a God-given blessing for me and for each of our members. We continue to reach out our hand to new members as Mark reached out to me.

By telling this story about JR, and about the Dads Group, I hope I am reaching out to you.

Jon Pavey

Marc William Douglas-Larrison

MAY 11, 1982 – SEPTEMBER 26, 2005

I'M RICHARD K. LARRISON. MY SON, MARC, PASSED AWAY ON SEP-
tember 26, 2005, in the burn unit of Wishard Memorial Hospital, where he was being treated for severe burns over eighty
percent of his body. Before I relate to you the circumstances
of Marc's death, how that experience has affected me, how
it brought me to the Dads Group, and what the Dads Group
means to me, I want to introduce you to my son.

Marc came to my wife Allyson and me one month shy of his third birthday. The courts had severed his biological parents' rights. He was lucky to have been removed from a negligent mother when he was three months old and placed in foster care. He, unlike a lot of children in the foster care system, did not get bounced from family to family. He was never returned to his parents who did not have the ability to care for him. He had been placed in the same foster home from the time he was three months old until the Indiana Department of Child Services decided that he should become our son. Marc did not like change, and the first few weeks with us were difficult for him. But it did not take him very long to adjust to his new family. He was the cutest little boy I had ever seen. His steel blue eyes could just about melt anyone, and he had the curliest blond hair. He also had a sense of humor that I did not know a three-year-old child could have. He was always doing something that would make you laugh. We always got the best service when we went to a restaurant, because he was a real charmer. He carried these traits throughout his life. His favorite thing to do was make people laugh, but I think that he later used humor to hide his internal anguish, depression and pains.

Marc also had a motor mouth. He was always talking—and had a hard time sitting still for any length of time. We had him tested and he was diagnosed with having Attention-Deficit/Hyperactivity Disorder (ADHD). When it came time for him to start school, we knew he would have difficulty in a traditional classroom. So, we enrolled him in a private Montessori School. After first grade we were able to get him enrolled in an Indianapolis Public School that taught using the Montessori method. This worked well for Marc, but he still had trouble staying quiet and on track. The doctor prescribed Ritalin for him and that helped him a lot.

Marc was very smart and breezed through school with very little effort. He did not have any problems in school until he was about fifteen years old. He had a very nasty breakup with a girlfriend and went through a period of extreme anger and frustration. One day Marc had a breakdown at school and the school counselor advised us to seek help for him at the Community North Mental Health Center, which we did. One of the psychiatrists at the Center diagnosed Marc as having Asperger's Syndrome. Which explained a lot of Marc's actions and social difficulties.

But also, Marc almost always complained of his joints hurting. The doctors thought that he was just suffering normal teenage growing pains. But Marc's pains seemed different than that to us. We took him to a rheumatologist and he diagnosed Marc as having the symptoms of fibromyalgia.

These two diagnoses, together—of Asperger's Syndrome and fibromyalgia—explained a lot of Marc's psychological and physical problems.

Marc spent about two to three months in classes and group sessions at the Mental Health Center before he went back to his normal high school. But he never really fit with any of the groups of kids at school and, at sixteen, begged us to take him out of school and teach him at home. Seeing how much school upset him, we agreed that we would try it. We gathered the necessary information and started down that road. After about a year of home schooling, Marc said, "I've had enough. I'm just going to take the GED and be done with it." We thought, "Okay, now Marc will get shown that he really does not know it all." To our surprise he passed the GED on his first attempt and he did it without even studying the GED book, guides, sample tests, etc. In fact, he came only a couple of points short of getting the GED with honors.

Marc still struggled with relationships and jobs. He was always happiest when he had a job, but he usually lost interest after a few months and would quit. He would then go into a period of depression where all he really wanted to do was stay in his room and play video games or watch movies. He left home when he was nineteen to live with a girlfriend. She kind of used Marc as her "boy toy," and I think Marc actually really did fall in love with her. When she was tired of him, she left him with a broken heart and some heavy debt. When Marc came back home at twenty-one, he was a different person. He was more tolerant of things. He was less angry and we thought that perhaps the year and a half on his own had taught him the life lessons that we could not. He started taking classes at Ivy Tech, and got— and kept—a job. He seemed to be getting his act together and trying to decide how he wanted to spend the rest of his life. He then got fired from his job because his boss thought he was lying and stealing, which Marc claimed he was not. I think it was Marc's Asperger's kicking up its heels and his boss not understanding Marc's actions.

Marc again entered a phase of depression and withdrawal. He did have a few friends, now, that he liked to hang out with. He would go to their houses to play video games and watch the WWF. One friend's wife was chronically depressed, and Marc told me he would never leave their house until he had made her laugh.

To summarize, Marc was a handsome and smart young man with steel blue eyes, blond hair and a charming personality. He had a great sense of humor and loved to make people laugh. He also had chronic pain from his fibromyalgia and had difficulty with establishing relationships, which is common with people who suffer with Asperger's.

Now that I have introduced you to Marc and the struggles that he had in life, I will tell you of the worst days of my life. It was about 1 a.m. on Monday, August 15, 2005, when we heard someone knocking on our front door. I got up, went to the door and found a police officer. He asked me if I knew a Marc Douglas-Larrison. I answered, "Yes, he is my son." The officer then told me that Marc had been in a single-car accident just south of our house. He said that Marc was up, walking and talking to the paramedics, and that they were going to be taking him to the hospital. He then left and said that someone would call us with more information in twenty to thirty minutes. I got Allyson up and explained all of this to her. We got dressed and waited and waited and waited. I finally got into the car and drove to where a police officer was blocking the road. I told him that I was Marc's father and wanted to know what hospital they had taken Marc to. He got on his radio and placed the query. The response was Wishard Memorial Hospital in Indianapolis. I went back home and got Allyson, and we went to Wishard. I let her out at the hospital door, and then parked the car in the parking garage and walked back to the door. Allyson was waiting at the door and said, "Rick, Marc is in the burn unit!" This was the first we knew that he had been burned. We went up to the burn unit to find out what was going on. The doctor met with us and told us that Marc had burns over eighty percent of his body with most being full thickness burns. He said that Marc had a fifty percent chance of surviving, but because of his age and the fact that none of his lung tissue had been burned, his chances were probably ten percent better than that. He also said that, on average, a person is in the burn unit one day for each percentage of their body that is burned. So, at best, Marc would be in the hospital for eighty days. Then we thought, "How did he get burned?"

The police officer had not said anything about him being burned, just that he had been in a single-car accident. We figured Marc had been driving too fast and had lost control of his car on the wet road, and that that was what had caused the accident. But, how did he get burned?

Allyson stayed at the hospital that night, and I came home to get things together, contact my boss, notify all of our family members of what had happened, and to shut down the retail portion of Allyson's website. I also went by where the accident had occurred, and to where Marc's car had been towed. I could not believe my eyes. His car was in the shape of the letter "H." The front bumper was nearly touching the firewall, and the back bumper was nearly touching the back window, and the car reeked from the smell of gasoline. The only door of the car that would open was the driver's door.

I then met with the police officer who was investigating the accident. He had found Marc's cell phone in the car and had looked at the call log. He found that the last calls Marc had made on the phone were to his friend Theresa, so he called her and questioned her about these last calls. Theresa told the officer that Marc had called her at about 10:30 Sunday night. Marc had sounded very upset and told her that he was going to kill himself. He said he was going to pour gasoline over his body and set himself on fire. If that did not kill him, he was going to pour gasoline in his car and drive it as fast as he could into her house. Theresa asked him why he wanted to hurt her and her family by driving into her house. Which Marc understood and agreed to not do. She also tried her best to tell Marc to talk to his mom and dad—that we would get him through his pain and get him whatever help he needed. They talked for seventy-two minutes and then again for another thirty minutes. [Later, after Marc died, I called Theresa and talked with her. She told me the things she had talked to Marc about that night. She had told him the right things for someone thinking about ending his life. She just could not talk him out of what he wanted to do.] I could not believe what the officer was telling me. Allyson had talked with Marc about suicide, and how it does not solve anything, and that sometimes it causes even worse problems. Marc had always had a dramatic streak and was too dramatic to commit suicide without leaving a manifesto. We had not found anything that stated his intentions. So, we felt that what Theresa had told the police officer, and what he had concluded, could not be right.

Marc did not die that night. Pouring the gasoline over his body and setting himself on fire only burned his skin. Pouring gasoline in his car and driving as fast as he could into something did not do anything but destroy his car, a utility pole, and a twenty-foot tall pine tree—ending up with the car wrapped around another tree. He walked away from that with only a minor bump on his head from hitting the windshield.

Somehow, Marc had endured all of this and survived. He got out of his car, took his driver's license, and started walking north. When he hit the utility pole, it had knocked the electricity out and probably made a horribly loud crashing sound. About a quarter of a mile from where Marc crashed his car is a volunteer fire station, which has a paramedic on duty 24/7. The fire chief, who lives next to the station, came out with a flashlight, trying to see what was going on. He heard moaning coming from across the road. He spotted Marc, helped him into the station, and got the paramedic up to help. Marc told them that he had been shocked. They immediately started treating Marc and paged the ambulance crew to get him to the hospital. They even discussed calling for the LifeLine helicopter, but decided they could get Marc to the hospital faster than getting the helicopter deployed.

They made the trip to Wishard in twenty minutes; a normal trip takes forty-five minutes.

Allyson's sister was living with us at the time all of this occurred. She worked close to the hospital and began dropping off Allyson on her way to work each day. I made arrangements to change my work schedule, so that I could arrive early and be able to leave again by 2:30 or 3. I would then go to the hospital to be with Allyson and check in on Marc. This would be our schedule until Marc was released from the hospital.

Marc progressed very well. Severely burned patients are usually on a ventilator until the last few weeks of their recovery. Marc was off of the ventilator and breathing on his own after about a week and a half. They were able to do some skin grafts, but most of his skin was going to have to be replaced with cultured skin. Marc had therapists working on him often. Several times I was in the room when they were there and Marc was helping them with the movements they had to do. I was very proud of him, because I could tell from his facial expressions that what they were doing was painful for him—but he still kept helping. Most of this time he was heavily sedated. One of the nurses told me they liked to keep the patients comfortable, but arousable. During one of the therapy sessions, he was more alert than usual and really helping the therapist. His eyes were open wider than usual and he seemed to actually be able to focus them. When they switched sides they were working on, I left to get Allyson so she could see how great Marc was doing. During the session, Marc was looking right at Allyson. She told him, "I love you, and am very proud of you." He mouthed, "I love you, too." Well, Allyson was just about doing back flips when she was coming down the hall after leaving Marc's room.

Marc's recovery continued on this positive progress until Sunday, September 25. That day, they were having troubles with his blood oxygen level, so they put him back on the ventilator and started doing tests to try to determine what was wrong. That night we got a call from the hospital saying they had determined that one of Marc's lungs had collapsed, but that they had been able to take care of it, and that he was resting comfortably. The next day, when Allyson got to the hospital, the nurse told her that she could not see Marc right then because they were doing tests on him. Allyson then heard a Code 99 (cardiac arrest) call to the burn unit. It was Marc. Allyson called me at 9 a.m. and told me about this, and said I needed to get to the hospital ASAP. When I got to the hospital, Allyson was in the family conference room with a chaplain, a counselor, and one of the interns. The intern was telling her that they had gotten Marc's heart going again, and that they were working on trying to see what was wrong. Shortly after that, they called another Code 99. The intern came back to tell us they had found a very fast-moving infection that had attacked Marc's heart before they were able to treat it—and that Marc had died. At that point we both just fell apart. We cried and held each other. I had to leave to call family members, friends, my boss, and I could call only one or maybe two before my emotions were to a point that I could not take anymore. I would have to go back to where Allyson was and hold her and get strength from her to make the next round of calls. At one point, the nurse came into the room to tell us that they had Marc ready for us to go see him, if we wanted to. Allyson said she did not think she could handle it. So, I went by myself to see Marc for the last time. It was the first time in forty-three days that I could touch him, and I hugged him and just cried. Before we left the hospital, Allyson finally did build her courage enough to go spend a few minutes with Marc, and of course I went with her. We held each other and touched our son for the last time and cried.

When everything was arranged for Marc's release from the hospital, we left and came home. Allyson was emotionally exhausted and wanted to lie down for a while. I needed to get out of the house to try to clear my head, so I went for a walk on our land. I went to one of the spots where Marc liked to go. I was surprised to find a little dome tent set up and one of his sleeping bags inside. Apparently, he would go out there at night to call his friends. I noticed something strange-looking on the ground, and picked it up. Then all of a sudden I realized what it was. It was part of Marc's underwear with his skin stuck to it. I had found the place where Marc had set himself on fire. What Theresa had said, and what the police officer concluded, were true! I instantly went into a tailspin and returned to the house to tell Allyson what I had found. I lay on the bed with Allyson for a while and just cried.

I am not a very emotional person. I lost my father in 1999 and hardly shed a tear. I lost my grandmothers a few years after that. Their loss was harder on me than losing Dad, but still very little tears. However, the loss of my son was devastating. Your child is never supposed to die before you do. That is backwards. The days after the death of a loved one are extremely hard. You have to make so many decisions and answer so many questions, when all you want to do is curl up in a ball. You have to decide how your son's remains are to be dealt with. You have to decide if you want a funeral or any other special service. We decided that we would have Marc cremated. Then we had to choose if we wanted a special urn. Marc loved dolphins. One of the urns was a very unique brass statue of two dolphins jumping out of the water. We felt that it was perfect, as it held true to Marc's spirit. So, that is the urn that we chose.

These tasks were extremely difficult on me. I felt empty, depressed, confused and I was in crisis mode. My company offers a service where employees can meet with a psychiatrist for free when they are having a life crisis. I called and got an appointment for the next possible opening. We told the doctor what had happened and she pulled out charts about grief and the grief cycle. No!!!!!! That is not what we want or need right now. We are in crisis mode. How do we get through today, tomorrow, and the rest of our lives? This psychiatrist did not have a clue as to what Allyson and I were going through, or what we needed from her. We left there feeling even more empty and disheartened.

Then we thought about someone who had helped Allyson's sister get through the loss of her husband. We called Marsha Hutchinson to make an appointment to talk with her. Marsha is a grief minister at St. Luke's Methodist Church. She met with us the very next day. She could not believe what the psychiatrist had done. She talked with us for about an hour or two. She told us about several grief support groups that were available. She talked about couples grief groups, but said she felt that the couples group did not offer enough support for the men. She said that men and women grieve in different ways, and that the men were not as open to discussing their feelings in the couples group. She told us about the moms grief group that meets at the church on Thursday evenings and the dads group that meets on Tuesday mornings at the Hilton. We said that, yes, those groups sounded more like something we needed. When we left the church that day we felt, "Finally, someone gets it.

Someone understands what we are going through and knows what others have found to help them adjust to their loss. "

Marsha gave my name and phone number to Steve Reed. Steve called me the next day to talk about the Dads Group and invited me to come for the next meeting. My first meeting with the Dads Group was on Tuesday, October 4. Just eight days after Marc's death. The first time a new dad comes to the group, we go around the table and each man tells his story of how he lost his son or daughter. When I told my story, and that Marc had died the previous Monday, every man around the table gasped. They could not believe I was coming to the meeting so soon after my loss. I was reared at a time when boys were taught not to show their emotions— and they definitely didn't cry. Boys and men who cry are looked down upon as not being very manly. I could not tell my story without crying, regardless of how hard I tried. To my surprise, Steve handed me a napkin to wipe my tears and placed his hand on my shoulder. He had been there himself, and had shed the tears himself, and it was okay. The same was true for every man around the table. They each know what you are feeling, and that what you need is someone to listen and offer reassurance that what you are feeling, they have felt, too. The first couple of times I told my story, I did not tell them that Marc had intentionally set himself on fire. I don't know if I was afraid of what they would think about Marc, or if I still was having difficulty in accepting what Marc had done. When I finally did tell Marc's entire story, I did not feel anything but empathy and understanding from these men. There are others in the group whose child took his or her own life, and they do understand.

In the group we often ask if anyone has ever felt this way or that way, and the answer is always, "Yes." No matter what you are feeling, someone around that table has had the same feeling. One day I asked if anyone was mad at God for taking their son or daughter. Adolf, our theologian, quickly answered, "It's okay to be mad at God. He can take it and he understands." Actually, I'm not "mad at God" for taking my son. I'm "mad at God" for giving us hope that Marc was going to survive—and then taking that hope away.

We come to breakfast every Tuesday morning, we place our sorrow and grief on the table for a while and feel we are around people who "get it!" When we leave, we each pick up our sorrow and grief, but it does not feel quite as heavy as it was when we put it down. We share a common bond. We feel like we are brothers and help each other through our difficult times. This was very much revealed to me when one of our members, Joe Leonard, passed away unexpectedly. Everyone in the group went to his showing and/or funeral. I stood by his casket and cried. This man was not related to me, and I had not known him that long, but his passing affected me more than the passing of my father. Joe had filled a hole in my heart and had shared a tear or two with me. Joe always had a smile on his face, and his face would light up whenever he talked about his son and/or daughter. The group misses Joe, and we talk about him occasionally. He would have enjoyed being a part of this writing venture and would have contributed an important story.

The group had very little laughter when I first joined. We would talk about our kids or how good or bad the Colts had played on Sunday. Or just about any other subject you can imagine. One week, I said that we had heard the stories of how our children had died. How about telling stories of how our kids had lived? What made them special or what they did that was really good. I think that we all got to know the real essence of each other's children that day. My story about Marc was how he loved to make people laugh. I also told them that Marc was a blond and absolutely loved blond jokes. After that, blond jokes started appearing in my email and sometimes they were delivered during the meetings. The laughter has a great healing effect and we all know that we can laugh again, and that it is safe to laugh in this group. The group is much more light-hearted now and the hour is usually filled with laughter.

The men in this group are very observant and they sense when someone is having a difficult time. Sometimes they recognize signs that a member is struggling even before the person who is suffering does. They offer support, are willing to listen, are not judgmental, and they let you know that what you are going through is a normal part of the healing process. Grief, especially from the loss of your child, is a roller coaster. You will have good days and bad days. Just being with these men, sharing a cup of coffee and perhaps a laugh or two, is enough to get me through the difficult times. I know that there are people who get through the loss of a child without the benefit of a support group. I just don't know how they do it.

Joining this group every Tuesday has helped me in more ways than I can ever express in words. These guys are my brothers and are a big part of who I have become since the loss of my son. My week is just not right without my Tuesday morning Dads Group fix.

Richard K. Larrison

Adam Toombs

November 29, 1989 – May 9, 2005

A FRIEND AND I WERE PULLING UP IN FRONT OF HER HOUSE AFTER an evening of dinner and conversation. My cell phone rang. A frantic voice screamed, "Dave! We are on our way to St. John's Hospital. Adam has quit breathing!!" I could hear the wail of an ambulance clearly.

As we left the Broad Ripple area of Indianapolis on our thirty-five-mile mission to Anderson, we eventually gathered our wits and tried to rationalize and project. "Perhaps he had choked on food...." "...Don't think the worst, it might be just another fluke trip to the emergency room." It then dawned

149

on me that my daughter, Cheyenne, was having a pool party that evening at a local natatorium.

In my heart of hearts, I sensed that the worst had happened.

The drive seemed a thousand miles long. I cried, prayed, grasped for hope, yelled, reasoned, rationalized … seemingly all at the same time. Over and over I kept saying, "This is not my call."

Cheyenne phoned. She was naturally distraught and crying. "Daddy, where are you?! They are taking Adam to the hospital!"

I assured her that I was on my way and did my best to comfort her.

Only three days before, Adam and I had gone to Conseco Fieldhouse to see the rookie sensation LeBron James and the Cleveland Cavaliers play the Indiana Pacers. This was also one of the last games we would have the opportunity to see Reggie Miller, as he was retiring after the season.

Every six months or so, Adam and I would find ourselves in a position and in the mood to have a good heart to heart talk about things that matter in life. That evening had begun with some light bantering between him and me over whether 58 percent was an acceptable free throw percentage. I asked him who was guarding him while he shot free throws. This argument usually ended with me playing the age, maturity and experience card. Besides, you gotta hit your free throws. An avid high school basketball fan, the most fundamental—yet to me most profound—of basketball truths was spoken so plainly by former Anderson High School Basketball Coach Norm Held. In a state that inspired the movie Hoosiers, Norm had built a tremendous program and had taken several teams to the state tournament finals. More than once in team booster club meetings he stated, "The game is free throws and lay ups."

Adam and I had talked about his college and career plans that evening. His plans would change from time to time as is normal with human beings. At one point in his life he had wanted to be a United Nations ambassador. At his core was a genuine and sincere desire for serving. On this particular night he was leaning toward being a lawyer and attending Indiana University. His plans included rooming with his best friend, Sam, so Adam could do his homework and help him make it through school.

Upon approaching the Anderson exit, a phone call came from my sister, who was frantic and wanting to know where I was. At this point I was starting to get emotional and asked if Adam was alive. She handed the phone to a nurse who assured me he was alive. I asked if he was brain dead ... by my calculations it had been about thirty-five minutes since the initial call. April 9, 2005, was about one week subsequent the passing of Terry Schiavo. Terry was the woman whose "right-to-life" was taken to task when they quit feeding her after years of being in a coma. This whole ordeal was fresh in my mind ... especially now.

The nurse relayed that she could not confirm any condition report. Adam was being prepped to be LifeLined by helicopter to an Indianapolis hospital. My heart sank. When we pulled up to the emergency room, I jumped out of the car and was ushered inside. As I walked through, I noticed that both sides of the hall were lined with young people. Adam's classmates. I was escorted to the cubicle and the curtain was drawn. There lay Adam, with a ventilator on—and a policeman on top of him frantically giving him compressions. Two or three doctors, a family friend, and Cheyenne and Adam's mother Pat, were all around the gurney. Pat looked at me and said, "It doesn't look good, Dave." Shock had set in with all of us. Her tone and demeanor was almost matter of fact.

A place was cleared for me beside the gurney. The policeman was a husky man probably about forty-five years old. I could sense the tremendous duress, both physically and emotionally, as the doctor directed his compressions. I said quietly to the officer, "God bless you."

The whole room seemed charged with 1000 volts of electricity.

As I stood by Adam's left side, commotion and controlled mayhem around me, Adam's limp hand kept falling off the table. I took hold of it and held it. His half-open eyes had lost their light. Periodically, the doctor directed the compressions to cease so that he could calibrate any vital signs. The monitor next to me would blip and then flat-line. The clock showed that it was 9:05 ... one hour since I had been phoned.

He was gone, but heroic measures continued.

It is odd how the whole incident, painful as it is, registered in my psyche details that imprint the memory. I just stared at Adam's face, a beautiful young man who only three short years ago had been short, rotund and rather slow afoot. He had used his savvy and determination to train himself into a competitive and competent soccer and basketball player.

Two weeks before, we had had Easter dinner at my brother's house and played our last one-on-one basketball game. He beat me mercilessly. This year he had come into his own physically and at last had come to the place where he consistently was beating me. He was 5'9" ... my height.

Oddly enough, a sense of gratitude came over me. I am a recovering alcoholic and there were some really hard years for him prior to my decision in 1999 to live a life of sobriety. There was a period of over a year where we had very little contact. When I chose a path of recovery, our relationship was restored. He and Cheyenne had been with me every anniversary that I received a token for sobriety. I was so grateful to God that I had good years with him. I could not have stood up against this adversity if it had not been for the tremendous gift of sobriety.

Nearly a thousand people attended the visitation, and the funeral home had to turn people away at the door eventually. It still took two and a half hours to clear the line. The funeral was held the next day at a local church. Once again nearly a thousand came to pay their respects.

As Adam's life was memorialized by the preacher, it brought many emotions and events to mind. His friends, family gatherings, his athletic endeavors and his own personal walk with God. The thought occurred to me, I am a blessed man to have been his father, a truly blessed man.

Toward the end of the service, the preacher shared my major issue with Adam ... his free-throw shooting. The mourners laughed.

To close the service, I chose to sing. It was all I had to offer Adam. When a friend asked me if it would be pressure, I told him, "You gotta hit your free throws."

I lead the congregation in a song that I had sung the Sunday morning we went to pick him up at the adoption agency, when he was two days old—the old hymn "Great is Thy Faithfulness." I shared my thoughts that I was honored to have been his father and that I would do it all again.

Playing at his funeral was such a blessing. I am so thankful that I was able to do that.

Then came life. Dealing with the loss.

As the shock wore off and reality set in, I knew that, as a recovering alcoholic, I had to face life on life's terms with the tools that had been given me. I stepped up attendance at recovery group meetings and shared openly and freely. It was helpful in dealing with some of the emotions. Few had experienced the death of a child, even fewer in sobriety. There was reluctance to talk about it.

At times things were okay, but other times waves of grief would overwhelm me, to the point of physical pain, like a deep aching in my bones. Added to the pressure of Adam's death were the questionable circumstances. As the story of the events leading up to the drowning unfolded, during the week of his funeral, issues were being raised that called for answers and accountability. Two days after his death, a long and painful process in search of those answers began. The ongoing investigation produced an intense anger that demands resolve but knows it will find none. My first reaction to such frustration used to be to drink, but the process of recovery had equipped me to deal with that situation. However, I had to find a way to deal with the anger.

It was nearly impossible to convey what was happening inside.

It was hard for those who had children, especially young children, to think about it. There were also well-meaning yet misdirected remarks about "God's will" or that Adam was "in a better place." Sometimes these encounters were bearable, but at other times they were useless and painful.

Terri Coe, the director of adult ministries at St. Luke's United Methodist Church, approached me on a Sunday morning after services, and in the course of conversation, mentioned that there was a men's grief support group on Tuesday mornings at a local restaurant. One of the church's pastors, Adolf Hansen, had been instrumental in starting and maintaining the group.

Again, my experience with recovery support groups had taught me to reach out for any available help. This seemed like a rather simple and helpful way to contribute to my own recovery from Adam's death.

You gotta hit your free throws.

The following Tuesday found me sitting in the hotel restaurant with a handful of men who shared the experience of having lost a child. None of these men knew me, none knew I was coming. Immediately, though, I knew I was in the right place.

This was the first time I could tell my story to people who could understand and empathize, who offered not contrived rhetoric, but genuine caring and concern. The meeting was an informal breakfast setting with no format. We just talked. They took the time to go around the table and each shared their own story. It occurred to me that, as horrible as it was for me, others' experiences were as painful and tragic. Some even more so.

Through the next several weeks, I found relief and comfort among men I barely knew. Though tragedy had brought us here, it felt as though God had handpicked this group to travel this path together.

Some weeks we individually share our experiences with grief. Other weeks we just talk sports, music or simply enjoy each other's company.

Perhaps the most significant lesson I have learned from this group is that it is acceptable and, in some cases necessary, to give myself plenty of room for personal expression of grief ... that there are no written rules, no mandates, no obligation to defend or justify feelings. It has also become clear that explanations to those who haven't experienced what we have, are futile.

The Tuesday morning men's grief support group soon became a lifeline to me. There was a period of time when I was unable to make the meeting regularly, but they made an effort to extend themselves and reach out their hands to me. In my mind I always know that there is a group of men who are willing to take time out of their lives for each other, for sharing and caring in an unexplainably genuine and healing way ... and that I am part of that group.

I truly am a blessed man.

Dave Toombs

Jeff Hamilton

December 5, 1972 – July 24, 2005

Where does one start in writing a story like this? Do you start at the beginning, in the middle, or at the end?

In my case, I feel I need to start in the middle.

It was a beautiful warm summer Sunday, the 24th of July, 2005. My wife Barb and I had spent this Sunday at church and had come home and enjoyed a leisurely lunch on the porch. The remainder of the day was spent reading and sunbathing by the pool, with an occasional dip to cool off. Late afternoon, we fixed our own snack for supper and fed Belle, our sweet and beautiful golden retriever. After reading the paper and finishing our dinner, we took Belle for her evening stroll. Later, I am watching a baseball game (the Cubs of course), and Barb is doing her Sunday routine with the pool, which includes checking water levels, chemical levels and general cleaning. The doorbell rings and I get up to answer the door and find two state troopers wishing to speak to both Barb and me. I call for Barb to come in, and I am pretty uneasy about this visit. They then break the news to us about Jeff's accident in South Carolina. We were told that it was a single-car accident, and that Jeff was by himself and did not survive. Of course, we are both in shock and looking for answers, and none are available.

The accident had happened around 2 a.m., but we did not find out until Sunday evening. We were told the troopers had come earlier in the day while we were at church and did not return until Sunday evening. One of Jeff's best friends, Mark, in Charlotte, was notified not long after the accident, but couldn't get in touch with us as it was to be done by the state police. What a lot of anxiety went through Mark and his wife Robbin on that terrible day. After recovering with some composure, we had to make the most difficult call of all, to Jeff's beautiful and wonderful sister Marnie. So very difficult because of how close Jeff and Marnie were—and Marnie's wonderful husband, and their three beautiful children, absolutely adored Jeff as well.

Friends and neighbors came over and stayed with us for a while, as we were trying to make plans to get to Charlotte as quickly as possible. We made arrangements early on Monday, dropped Belle off at the vet, and headed to the airport. We had a mid-morning flight and, after several delays, finally arrived in Charlotte early Monday evening. In the meantime, I was making phone calls to the coroner's office and the funeral home, and Marnie was talking with the minister at their church, which we would visit while in Charlotte. It is amazing as to what one can do when in such a state of shock. Friends and relatives are being notified by so many. One phone call would take place and this would trigger a chain reaction of more calls being made.

On Tuesday, the arrangements are being made as we meet with the funeral home, the church, and the cemetery. Sadly, we were already familiar with the funeral home and the cemetery, as Marnie had lost a child after a difficult pregnancy. We also had gotten to know the senior pastor of their church, as we had attended there several times. Again, while in somewhat a state of shock, we were able to make plans and arrangements for the viewing, the service and the burial. Everything was delayed until Thursday evening, with so many coming from out of town. With Marnie and her family in Charlotte, there was a place to gather. The home was always full of food, family, and friends, and it continued day and night.

There were friends and relatives from Montana, Texas, New York, and from all over the Midwest and the South. We were told by the funeral home that they had never seen so many floral arrangements, and that they had to open up extra rooms for the ones that had come to the receiving. So many of Jeff's friends there were all dressed up. They said they didn't want to embarrass Jeff, as he was always dressed "just so"—hence the nickname "JAZZY." Also, no one wanted to leave, and many stayed later than normal that evening at the funeral home.

Friday was a rainy day, and people started showing up at the church with umbrellas and raincoats. The church was full and the music was playing. The music was some of Jeff's favorite recorded songs. One of Jeff's friends had taken some of Jeff's CDs to make the recording. Then the service started, and what a beautiful service. Friends spoke as well as Jeff's mother. It has always marveled me as to how close Barb and Jeff were. "Are." I have known many wonderful families and mothers with sons, but I have never witnessed a relationship between a mother and son like Barb and Jeff. The smiles on both faces were *electric* when they saw each other—especially if it was sometime like in the spring when there were no college football games to attend. Barb spoke of this relationship and about Jeff's personality: quiet, shy, and very caring of others. Again, in speaking of Jeff's "Jazzy" appearance, one of his friends mentioned a story to the full church about the time his appearance and hair had to be just so—and this was just to go play basketball! Another friend said that he hoped his shirt and tie went with his suit, as he didn't want Jeff to be disappointed. As the service ended, the rain had stopped and the sun came out. This was only fitting, as his mother's nickname for him was "Sunshine." A long procession to the cemetery with a brief service. Many returned to the church for conversation, hugs, and prayers.

While still in a state of shock, we now must take care of the estate and settlements. After a quick trip back to Indy, and then back to Charlotte, this process started. Jeff had been planning to leave for Chicago and had already cancelled his apartment lease in Charlotte. The apartment complex was so gracious, as they gave us another month to move and close out utilities, and did not charge for the month. We had to work with the probate office, and North Carolina laws, and this was not easy. There was insurance to deal with, Jeff's employer (Wachovia), bank accounts, retirement accounts, etc., and what to do with Jeff's personal belongings. Mostly everything was taken to Marnie's or back to Indianapolis. Some very meaningful items were given to Jeff's friends as they asked for them—a baseball cap to one, a T-shirt to another, CDs and beer mugs to others.... Jeff had had his favorite Christmas music, recorded by his favorite artists, on a CD, which his mother still plays during the holidays.

"The beginning" of Jeff's story came about on the 5th of December, 1972, with Jeff arriving seven weeks early. With a difficult pregnancy, early delivery, and Jeff being in the hospital for about a month, I look back and can say that we are very thankful to have had Jeff with us for as long as we did.

What a delight Jeff was to raise and watch grow from a newborn into a wonderful young man. One looks back and wonders where the time and the years go. A special remembrance is of Jeff and Marnie growing up together, as they were only two years apart. A special story of Jeff was when he was two. Jeff had to wear corrective shoes when he was little and, with these being Stride Rite, they were quite expensive. Not long after he had his first pair, the toe of each shoe was worn through. They were exchanged and then again; the toe of each shoe was worn through on the second pair. The store manager, of course, was quite puzzled and wanted to know about Jeff's activities. Being all boy, he played hard and rode his tike bike fast down the incline of our driveway. Needless to say, the shoes were his brakes as he made the turn! I also remember, traveling back home to visit family, Jeff would have his matchbox cars spread out around the backseat. The cars would go flying every time I stopped. Marnie would climb out of her seat to pick them up for him. And I remember Marnie walking home from school, and Jeff waiting in the wooded backyard with "six-shooters" on to protect Marnie from the Indians. As a neighbor pointed out, the Indians never got her. Growing up, Marnie would help with homework and they would ride the bus together and, to this day, many mutual friends stay in touch with Marnie. Watching

Jeff play sports was especially exciting, fun, and of course, filled with heartache. Jeff played sports from Little League baseball and Little League football through high school varsity sports. The highs were with the fun with his teammates, to the lows of losing in the semi-state of the state high school basketball tournament. Marnie happened to be Jeff's most vocal cheerleader and critic as well. With Marnie it might have been, "What did he swing at that pitch for?" Or if he hit one of his "sweet" jump shots, she would get all excited.

One of the reasons that kept Marnie and Jeff so close would be the moves made through the years. It seemed like things would be settled and then a transfer would take place. While Marnie and Jeff were growing up, I think their longest time in any one school system was four years. Fortunately, the last two moves kept Marnie and Jeff in close touch and driving distance to their friends.

When Marnie left for college, they stayed in touch via the phone and with mutual friends, and Jeff had a place to stay when he would go visit. It always marveled Barb and me as to how close the two were and how much they enjoyed each other. This always made for pleasant vacations and trips to visit the families. When they both were at the same university, it helped, as we would get to see both for the football, fraternity, and sorority weekends.

After graduation, Jeff was searching for his right path, as most do at a young age. With our children and grandchildren (Jeff's nephews and niece), now living in Charlotte, we were together again as much as possible. Marnie was now married with these three little ones, Austin, Matthew, and Gracie. To them he was just plain "Uncle." My how the grandchildren loved Jeff, and how he loved them. Jeff was never too busy to build something, play a game, or read a story.

Jeff decided to make a career change and relocate to his favorite city, Chicago. With many friends and a special girl friend already there, and INDY being near Chicago—and Marnie and her family loving Chicago as well—this would be great for all. Everyone was so happy for Jeff, and it would be great for easy visits to any of the cities.

Then the tragedy struck and the world came crashing down.

We have been to the middle, then the beginning, and now the end, when the healing process starts.

Upon returning to Indianapolis and back to work, we were looking for something and not sure what. The faith is very strong, but there was not the healing process for grief from our church that we felt we needed, so we looked elsewhere. It was surprising, in that we are members of a very large church with many ministers on staff. No one reached out to us, which we still do not understand. Since Jeff's accident, and us voicing our concern to the church, this is now changing. One comforting aspect of our faith: we knew that we would be together again.

We were told through one of the local hospitals about grief counseling, which we tried. The meetings were okay, but I was the only male, and the group was about a loss of a spouse. Even though the meetings were meaningful, there was something missing when we were the only ones with a lost child. We kept looking, and I chose not to do professional help, as I wanted to work through this my own way.

Old friends did not know what to say, and new friends were sought out. All of the old friends and relatives would shy away from the subject about Jeff and kind of feel uncomfortable in conversations. With new friends and acquaintances, it was like, "Really? What happened? How did you react? What kind of person was Jeff?" The new people did not know Jeff and wanted to know more about him and how we managed. I would tell them about Jeff and his love for his family and friends, and even for people he didn't know— like through his volunteer work for Habitat for Humanity. I would tell them about his style of dress and workout ethic. Then I would just say, "Hey, go to www.mem.com and read the tributes." Many would respond after reading these tributes and were like, "Wow."

One day Barb tells me about this dads group that she had seen an ad for in a supplement part of the paper that I normally don't read. I didn't pay much attention and didn't think anymore about it. The ad appeared again a couple of weeks later, and Barb pointed it out to me again. I thought, "What the heck," and called the number. It was an answering machine and so I left a message. Later, I get a return phone call from Mark Fritz, one of the Dads Group members, and am invited to come the next Tuesday morning for coffee. Not knowing what to expect, but knowing I needed something, I decided to go.

With some apprehension, I made the first Tuesday meeting and was introduced by Mark, as he was the one who had placed the ad and then returned my phone call. The ones who were there went around the room and told their stories about their loss and the circumstances involved. There were stories of every kind, and the fathers were from all walks of life. I felt a connection and decided to return the following Tuesday.

Since then, I will miss the Tuesday mornings only if I am out of town, and then will adjust my schedule when possible to avoid missing. The first winter, I was the only one to show up on a day when a snow storm had blanketed the city. I spent the hour in the lobby listening to the travelers figure out how they were going to deal with the storm and then left for the office.

I remember, not long after I had started going and had listened to some of the stories, how fortunate I felt to have had Jeff with us for as long as we did, and for the wonderful life with him. The stories are very tragic, and some with lengthy addiction problems, and I made a comment about this. Kim, a member of the group, said, "Marv, the journeys have all been different, but the destination is the same." That is why we are here: to help one another with the grief and share our experiences. My how these guys do "get it."

This was in the spring of 2006 and, as I said, I don't miss a Tuesday morning unless I am out of town. This is a wonderful collection of men who can laugh and cry, poke fun at each other, and then tell each other goodbye, wish each other a good week and see you next Tuesday. Some Tuesdays there may be sixteen at the Hilton, or maybe only four will show up. Again, we all want to know how each other is doing or what is going on in their lives. Once in a while we will get together for an evening with our spouses joining us. These gatherings may be at someone's home, a clubhouse, or out to dinner. These are always wonderful social gatherings, and they give the spouses a chance to meet the others as well.

The best part of the group is that someone is always there to help if needed. This may be with conversation, a fundraiser, or any other need that may arise. Even though we see each other on Tuesdays, e-mails and phone calls get exchanged throughout the week. One can sense when someone is really down, or dealing with issues, and will be there to pick him up.

After almost three years, I am not sure where I would be without the Tuesday morning Dads Group. I just know in my heart that the "therapy" that I receive from the group is more meaningful to me than professional counseling. Also, the friendship cannot be measured. The strong faith of seeing each again keeps me going.

I guess I have come to the conclusion of my story. I miss Jeff every day, but I know that he is always with us. Whenever I see a beautiful butterfly, I know I have company. I have seen them on my windshield in Chicago in the wintertime during a snow storm, and fluttering around my golf ball before I sink a long putt. One of Jeff's favorite songs is "Collide," by Howie Day. One time, I am in Germany on a business trip, and walk into a pub in Cologne with friends, when this song starts to play. I am thankful for the time we had together as a family and the cherished memories we still carry with us each day. And I am thankful that there is something of Jeff in each of Marnie's children—whether it is the smile, the athleticism, the style of dress, or especially the caring of others. One time, after the accident, I didn't want to be in a family picture while on vacation. I didn't want to be there without Jeff. But then I realized this wasn't fair to Barb or to Marnie and her family. With Jeff being in each of the grand-children, the "chain" is never broken. We still do the family pictures during the holidays and on vacation, with me being included. And we know that Jeff is there, too.

It is this closeness to Jeff, my family, my strong faith, and my relationship with the Tuesday morning group that help sustain me and keep me going each day in the continued healing process. I truly am a blessed man.

To you, Jeff, I am so proud to call you my son, and I miss you so very much.

Marvin Hamilton

Jake and Travis Findley

JAKE OCTOBER 31, 1994 – FEBRUARY 3, 2007
TRAVIS JULY 1, 1997 – FEBRUARY 4, 2007

LIFE IS GOOD...

The week of Christmas, 2006, our family finally had the chance to take a long-promised vacation together. We had taken vacations with other families, and had gone on short trips to Kings Island, but we had never taken a real vacation just as a family.

Jake was twelve and Travis was nine, and when we asked them where they wanted to go, they said somewhere warm with a beach. We all loved the ocean and warm weather, so my wife, Becky, and I started looking into vacation deals. We decided on Paradise Island in Nassau, Bahamas. The boys lit up with excitement when we showed them pictures of where we were going. This was going to be a very special vacation. I could feel it deep inside of me.

Early that Christmas morning, after we opened presents and had our Christmas celebration, we packed up the car and headed to the airport. Travis was all smiles and Jake had this little grin that said he was excited, too. Both tried to contain their excitement as we made our way through security and headed to our gate.

Life was good. I felt all my dreams were coming together. Becky was a wonderful wife and a phenomenal mom. She had poured her heart and soul into the boys since the day they were born. I loved how our family was growing and bonding. I had a good job and Becky worked part-time and was able to work her schedule around the boys' schedules, so she would always be there in the morning to get them on the bus and again in the afternoon when they got home. We belonged to a terrific church and our faith in God was becoming stronger and an important foundation in our lives. The boys were growing up fast and becoming young men with personalities and character that were far beyond their years.

Our lives revolved around the boys and we wouldn't have wanted it any other way. I coached the boys' basketball and baseball teams, and we made it a priority to be at every game and school activity—so weeks and weekends were packed. Life was busy, but a good kind of busy. This was the life Becky and I had dreamed about. God had truly blessed us with two extraordinary boys who blessed our lives beyond our expectations and dreams. Life was good and we did not take it for granted.

Later that Christmas night, we arrived in the Bahamas, got something to eat at the hotel, and took a walk outside by the pool. We could hear the waves crashing on the beach just a few yards away and the seagulls singing as they flew in the night sky. It was music to our ears. This was going to be a time to relax and enjoy our time together as a family, just the four of us.

The vacation was *awesome*. The first day was a beautiful perfect sunny day with temperatures in the 80's. Jake, Travis and I got up early and took a walk on the beach. We had just bought a new camera so I brought it along and took all my scenery shots and a bunch of great pictures of the boys. We rented jet skis later in the day while Becky hung out at the pool. We had a blast. Travis had such a great time that he wanted to do it the next day as well. I thought, "We're on vacation, why not?!" So we did it again the next day, and Travis was being quite the daredevil. He was driving and had it wide open a couple times as we were flying and bouncing across the waves. He was laughing the whole time, loving every second of it. When we were done, Jake had his orange and black football ready for us to play catch. Of course, I was stopping them every once in awhile to take another picture with the best background I could find—whether the ocean, a palm tree, the pool, or whatever. It was uninterrupted time with my boys and I was taking it all in.

Our family had fun no matter what we did, and the time in the Bahamas was special, as we knew it would be. We were smiling, laughing and enjoying being together. It was something I knew would be etched in my memory for the rest of my life.

I had no way of knowing that in a little over a month, my life was going to change in a sudden and drastic way, and never be the same again.

Our world is changed forever.

It was February 3, 2007, a cold but very clear and sunny day for the early part of February. It was the day before the Super Bowl—Super Bowl XLI, between the Indianapolis Colts and the Chicago Bears. Living in Greenwood, Indiana, a few minutes south of Indianapolis, our family was excited about the Colts finally having the chance to win the Super Bowl. The Colts had been knocking on the door for several years, and had finally beat the New England Patriots in the AFC Championship game, to play on the ultimate stage. You could feel the buzz in the air as the entire Indianapolis area was ready to rock.

We had the whole day planned for the Super Bowl the next day. It would be a day of going to church in the morning, coming back home and getting all of our snacks ready for the game, and watching the pre-game festivities. Jake wanted me to make Hooters hot wings, and Becky and Travis wanted some of Becky's tasty monkey bread.

Around 11 a.m. Becky and I ran out to get all the things we needed for the next day. The boys stayed home and played Playstation. While we were in Meijer, Becky and I ran into the mother of our friends who were coming over for pizza later that night. She told us that her grandson had a game at 1:15 p.m. and invited us to come. When we got home, we told the boys about the game and decided to go. After the game, the boys were invited to go home with these same friends who were coming over that night. Since they had recently moved into a new house, their son, who was the same age as Travis, wanted the boys to come over and play pool. We said some quick goodbyes on the way out, and said we would see them in a few hours.

Becky and I went home. Since Becky had had knee surgery at the beginning of January, she went to our upstairs game room to use a CPM (continuous passive motion) machine to get some movement in her knee. I stayed downstairs and watched NFL Network to pass the time until everyone came back to our house for pizza. They had planned to get to our house at 5:30 p.m. or so.

A little after 6 p.m. Becky yelled from upstairs, "Do you think you should give them a call? They should have been here by now." I said they were probably getting the pizza and I would wait a little longer. Another ten to fifteen minutes passed by and she told me I really should give them a call. I ran upstairs to talk to her and, while we were talking, the phone rang. I looked at the caller ID and it said "Community South," which is one of our local Indianapolis hospitals. I thought, "What in the world. Why would Community South be calling?" I will never forget the chilling words on the other end of the line when a sheriff's deputy identified himself and said, "Are you the parents of Jacob and Travis Findley?" I answered, "Yes, why?" He responded, "There's been an accident...." My heart sank and I replied, "Is everyone okay?" He said, "You will have to talk to the emergency personnel, but you need to come right away."

I believe it was at that moment I went numb, but tried to remain calm as I told Becky what he had said. I could see the worry and distress in her eyes. We got in our car and took that drive that seemed like a drive straight to the gates of hell. We kept thinking, "How did they know it was our boys?" They weren't carrying any ID on this particular day. Maybe they were okay and had told the nurses who they were. Maybe it wasn't anything to panic about. What kind of accident? We didn't know anything. We were just praying and hoping that they were okay.

Since Becky was using crutches, I pulled up to the emergency room doors and let her out. She went ahead while I parked the car. As I was making my way to the door, a sheriff's deputy met me and had a look on his face that didn't need words. But I was still hoping. As I walked in, there were several emergency room nurses standing nearby. I looked around but didn't see the boys anywhere. Becky was given a chair, so she would be more comfortable, and the main nurse started talking to us. She was describing all the occupants of the vehicle. Then she started describing Jake, saying he was about twelve or thirteen, and asked us, "Was he wearing braces?" We said yes, and then she said the words that will haunt us forever. *He didn't make it.* Becky screamed and cried at the same time with the worst look on her face that I had ever seen. Our Jake was gone. I went completely numb. My body shut down. I did not cry, but my insides were screaming to say it wasn't real or true, and I had the most intense agonizing feeling I had ever had in my life. I managed to ask the nurse, "What happened?" She said, "The van that they were riding in was hit by a train." I couldn't believe it. "A train?!" "Where did this happen?" She told us that it was by Stones Crossing Road, a crossing that didn't have any gates or lights. I couldn't believe what I was hearing. How could this have happened? Then she told us that we needed to identify Jake's body. Becky said she couldn't go in there yet. I thought, "Oh my God, what is Jake going to look like from this type of accident?" I didn't want to do it. I didn't want to go in that room and see him lying on a hospital table. Dead. It was only a few hours earlier that we had been having such a good time, excited about watching the Super Bowl the next day.

I slowly walked in, and there he was, with no life, lying on the hospital table with a neck brace. But, amazingly, with no signs otherwise of the accident he had just been in. He looked peaceful. I wanted him to look at me and say he was okay. This was final, but I couldn't comprehend it in that moment.

Another nurse walked in with me, and she was crying pretty emotionally. She told me that she had a twelve-year-old son, and just couldn't imagine, and said how sorry she was. I was still numb and couldn't believe I wasn't crying, but your body does strange things in traumatic situations. Becky finally came in, and we stood there together, in shock. We told Jake how great he was, and how much we loved him. We didn't want to leave, but the other nurses came in and told us that Travis had been taken to Methodist Hospital in downtown Indianapolis, and that he was critical. We were in such shock about Jake, that we hadn't thought to ask about Travis. The chaplain on duty that night offered to drive us, because they all knew we were in no state of mind to drive.

As we were going out the door, Becky looked at one of the nurses and asked, "Is my other baby going to die, too?" We found out later, that the accident had happened right around 5:15 p.m. Forty-five minutes after that, was when Becky first told me that I should give them a call because they were late. A mother's instincts should never be questioned. She had obviously felt that something was not right.

When we got to Methodist Hospital, we made our way to the emergency room area and a doctor met us. I immediately asked him, "What are his chances?" He responded, "Slim. He's very critical." Becky and I looked at each other and didn't say a word. The doctor took us to the room where they were working on Travis. He had probably six or seven, maybe more, nurses and doctors working on him feverishly. As with Jake, Travis didn't look too bad. Becky and I started talking to him, but he didn't respond to our voices. We knew right then, there wasn't much of a chance for him either. My mind was reeling. "What in the world is happening?" "Could we be losing both our sons in one night?" I could not stand the thought, and started praying silently. There wasn't anything else to do.

Becky and I went back to the waiting area, as family members and the pastor whom Becky worked for had quickly made their way to Methodist. We immediately grabbed hands and prayed together. Every chance we had, we would grab hands and pray. It was so powerful. I knew there was nothing else we could do in those moments, but give it all to God and let Him take care of whatever was going to happen with Travis.

A neurologist confirmed our worst fear when he did some tests on Travis. He came to the waiting area with more words that will haunt us forever. *He has sustained an unsurvivable injury.* They worked well past midnight on Travis, but he was finally gone. There were still friends, family and a pastor there until Travis was pronounced dead. A friend of ours, Steve Rhoades, said, "Heaven is a little bit sweeter now." I will never forget how he said that. Even though I was devastated, those words took the edge off a little, at least for a couple seconds. I looked at my dad and asked, "We've prayed all night, let's do something different?" Steve suggested maybe singing a song. I said, "Perfect." I asked my dad, "What song should we sing?" He said without hesitation, "How about 'Amazing Grace'?" I said again, "Perfect." So we all held hands, and made a circle around Travis, and sang "Amazing Grace." This was when the tears came for me, but I sang anyway. It was like we were all sending Travis up to be with the Lord.

Reality and shock...

Becky and I now had to hold onto each other and go home.... The home we had watched the boys grow up in ... the home in which we had played together, prayed together, watched movies together, watched sports together, talked to each other, laughed together, and most importantly, bonded and grew so close as a family. All of that was now gone, never to be the same, never to be replaced.

Just two weeks earlier Jake and I had been watching the AFC Championship game between the Colts and the Patriots. When the Colts came back and won, Jake and I were so pumped, jumping up and down and high-fiving, hugging, yelling and running around the house.... ...Just over a month earlier the four of us had had our Christmas vacation in the Bahamas.... And now all of that was gone. *No more playing catch in the backyard with my boys, no more basketball games out in the driveway, no more football in the backyard, no more stories at night. ...No first dates, no seeing them get their driver's licenses, no watching them graduate from high school, no watching them go off to college, no congratulating them on getting their first job, no watching them marry the girl of their dreams, no grandkids ... no carrying on the Findley name.* All gone in a flash!!

When Becky and I walked in the house, the silence was deafening. My mind was both in a constant state of a whirlwind of emotions ... and I felt completely numb. *No more looking in at them while they are sleeping, knowing they are safe and sound. No more late night visits in our bedroom after a bad dream or getting sick.* The silence was too much to handle. Becky and I didn't sleep at all. We sat up in bed talking all night, but we really didn't know what to do or how to feel. I kept expecting Travis to run into our room. We had to walk by both of the boys' rooms to get to our bedroom and it was excruciating each and every time. Seeing all their stuff ... hearing nothing coming from their rooms ... and knowing it would ALWAYS be silent. The worst night of our lives, and we didn't know what to do. We knew only that we would have to get up the next morning and start planning our sons' funeral.

The next morning did not go as we had planned the night before. Shortly after we got up, the phone started ringing and neighbors, friends and church members were ringing our doorbell. It started out fast and didn't let up until later that night. We could not believe the outpouring of love and support from everyone around. We had enough food to feed the entire neighborhood. We didn't have much of an appetite, but we felt so grateful. The phone did not stop ringing that entire day, or for the next month.

Then there was the media. I was leery about letting the media into our house and into our lives. But something inside me said, *"Do this for the boys. Talk about what great blessings they were and be positive about this. Show that faith can overcome even the most devastating circumstances on earth."* So that's exactly what I did and, to be fair, the media did an outstanding job of showing the expressions of kindness, and not airing just another tragedy that had taken place that day. Little did I know, the media would play a big part, in the coming months, in helping us to triumph over tragedy.

Our church, Mount Pleasant Christian Church, was nothing but amazing as they were there for us day and night no matter what the circumstance involved. Becky and I will be forever grateful to all the pastors, members and staff for their faithfulness, love, encouragement and support that shined a light on us and gave us hope in the darkest days. We owe a special debt of gratitude to Senior Pastor Chris Philbeck and his wife Sandy, and Connections Pastor Rich Green and his wife Patty. They prayed with us, counseled us, ministered to us and were simply friends when we needed friends the most. They will forever have a place in the depths of our hearts.

The next few weeks were a nonstop barrage of phone calls, hundreds of letters and cards received each day, and constant visits from people who wanted to do whatever they could to help us. So many people showed that they cared. It was incredible and amazing, and Becky and I will never forget the love of our community, our friends, and especially our family and church family.

Men and emotions…

The next few months were extremely difficult for me. I had a constant aching in my stomach, kind of like a sick feeling, that never seemed to go away. I felt sadness, devastation, hopelessness, anger, denial, and some peace. I didn't know what my purpose was anymore. I had lived for those two boys, and my personal goals had centered on them—to be a good dad, to teach them right from wrong, to teach them about faith in God, to teach them about sports. To be a huge part of their lives. It was all gone now, and I felt helpless and hopeless. *What do I do now?* I knew I would never be able to replace that hole in my life no matter what I did. At times I felt like I couldn't go on. *How could I live without those two precious boys who meant so much to me? How could I ever function again the way I normally do?* There was a constant churning of thoughts and feelings, and I didn't know how to control them. I didn't know how I was going to cope. I couldn't focus at work and the stress levels went way up. I battled thoughts of the accident and wondered if they had seen the train coming. I wondered what the impact must have been like. I wondered if they had suffered.

On my forty-five-minute drives to and from work, I con-stantly prayed and thought about the boys. I would some-times cry all the way to work or all the way home. If I wasn't praying, I would listen to loud rock and roll or Christian music to get me through. I could be at my desk working, and start tearing up thinking about a memory of the boys.

It had all happened too fast. I, too, had put my heart and soul into those boys since the day they were born, and promised myself I would never take them for granted. And I never did. But the boys were here one day and then gone the next. *How can your life change in just seconds?* Every time I looked at their pictures, I would shake my head in disbelief. It didn't seem real. It seemed impossible.

Where to turn…

I knew I would need some sort of counseling to help me deal with these emotions. Our church set Becky and me up with Woody Church, a compassionate counselor with a biblically-based approach. I needed this type of counseling that gives hope, but men and women grieve differently, and Becky realized she needed a different counselor to help her with the emotions and feelings she was going through. I respected that, but continued to go to the same counselor.

My counselor helped me look at eternal things rather than temporary things. He showed me a verse that I hold on to each and every day. It is Romans 8:18 and it says, *"I consider that our present sufferings are not worth comparing with the glory that will be revealed in us."* This verse means to me that no matter what we go through here on earth—even if it's the most tragic thing in the world like losing a child—we won't even remember how we suffered, once we get to heaven and are reunited with our loved ones. How awesome is that promise? So, I really leaned on the Bible for strength, comfort and hope.

But even as helpful as my counselor was, and even with all the consoling passages he gave me, I realized he didn't really know how I felt, because he hadn't been through it. I needed an outlet to sort through my feelings and figure out how to deal with them, but I didn't know what the answer was. I was confused about faith and why God would let this happen. I asked God all the time in my prayers why this happened. Why those two precious boys? Why, why why? None of it made any sense. But I knew He was with me, and taking care of me day by day, as I tried to move forward.

Honoring Jake and Travis

Becky and I both were simply crushed. Life had been so good, and was going as we had always dreamed, and now this. We couldn't leave it like that ... with death. As a way to help us take a step forward, we needed to honor our boys and their lives. We wanted to do something that could save lives in the future. So we decided to use the contributions, from the hundreds of letters and cards we had received, to start The Jake and Travis Findley Special Fund Account. If we could get enough money raised, we were hoping to fund upgrades at the crossing where the accident had happened—and prevent other families from ever experiencing the unimaginable pain we were going through.

We knew it was a long shot, but we had to give it a try. And the community was right there with us. Two men in particular—Brady Clements and Jim Copp—had some ideas of their own, and the result was the creation of The Jake and Travis Arms of Life Fund. We will always feel immense gratitude for Brady and Jim—and I could not do justice in describing how God put His hand on this effort. Within nine months, enough money was raised through the Arms of Life to upgrade the crossing where the accident took place, and to upgrade two others with flashing lights and cross arms. A fourth crossing is still being considered at the time of this writing. Each of these crossings was very dangerous but are now much safer with these upgrades due to the sacrifice Jake and Travis made—along with a loving community in and around Indianapolis, and even throughout the country, that wanted to make a difference. [To read more about the Arms of Life and see some pictures and videos of Jake and Travis, visit www.armsoflife.com.]

Jake and Travis' school friends—teachers and students alike— wanted to honor them, too, as a step forward. In the spring of 2007, Sugar Grove Elementary School—where Jake had attended kindergarten through fifth grade, and where Travis had attended until the latter part of third grade—created an award to honor the boys and recognize a fifth grade student for his character and qualities that were part of the Sugar Grove Pledge of Excellence. Their great tribute to Jake and Travis, The Findley Award for Excellence, means so much to each year's recipient.

The fact that the boys have been honored by their school, and their peers, is tremendously meaningful to Becky and me. It is comforting to know that others valued individual characteristics in each of them, just as we did.

Jake was the great encourager. He had a great love for younger kids and would go out of his way for them and encourage them when they needed it. At Travis' basketball games, whenever there was a timeout, Jake would be the first one there to pat kids on the back and say good job, or after an exciting win he would be jumping up and down celebrating with them and picking them up in a big bear hug. At Travis' baseball games, he would be our designated batboy, but he was so much more than that. When one of the kids would strike out and get upset, Jake would be right there putting an arm around him, saying it was okay. He would be full of encouragement so they could go out and try to get a hit the next time up. No matter if it was a good game or a bad game, I know Jake made a big difference in the way the kids felt.

Jake's friends loved his laugh, his love for football, his taste in music, his talent on the guitar and his signature trademark of always wearing a hat. It was usually a blue North Carolina Tar Heels hat or a red Ohio State hat. Later, he would proudly wear his Colts hat every chance he had. Jake had a huge heart and tried to be nice to everyone he met.

Travis also had a huge heart. He had a beautiful smile and a contagious laugh. He loved animals and wore sports jerseys almost every day. He had a talent for sports and was a natural at almost anything he tried. His first love was basketball, but baseball wasn't too far behind. The following are things Travis' classmates said about him:

"He always had a smile on his face."

"Travis always told you how good you were doing."

"He was always caring and respectful."

"You could beat him up and he wouldn't even get mad."

"When we get in arguments at recess, he never yelled. He'd just stand there and wait until the fight was over."

"One day I left early and forgot my homework and math book. Travis brought it to me and I didn't even ask him to."

"We had a new little girl in the third grade, which was not even in our room. She was sitting by herself at recess. Travis went up to her and asked if she was new and asked her to play."

"At lunch, there's only supposed to be four people on one side of the table. One day, there were five on a side. Travis said he was

the last person to sit down. He wasn't, but he got up and moved anyway."

"Travis never cheated."

"Travis never lied."

I didn't know some of these things about Travis until he was gone, but they didn't surprise me.

In my opinion, Jake and Travis were angels sent down to be on earth. I just didn't know it was going to be for such a short time.

Tony Dungy and our common thread

Sometimes we cross paths with someone in the most unexpected ways. When I had the chance to meet Tony Dungy, I had imagined that it would be an opportunity to meet one of the most respected men not only in football, but in life itself, and that he would be able to give me some guidance, since he had been through a similar tragedy of his own a year earlier when he lost his son James. What I hadn't imagined is that we would develop a close friendship that would last a lifetime. His focus on the positive, and his belief that God can get you through anything, will hold firm with me for the rest of my life. I will be forever grateful for his friendship—and for the friend and third grade teacher who brought him into my life.

Sometimes we don't know what to expect from God, but I truly believe He gave me this opportunity. I got a call one day from Travis' third grade teacher, Linda Gallman. She loved Travis and did some remarkable things to keep his spirit alive during the rest of the school year after the accident. One day, she said, "Chuck, we have been in contact with Tony Dungy." She then proceeded to tell me that my friend Scott Snyder had written to Tony, telling him of the accident. She said that Tony had received the letter when he returned from the Super Bowl, that he was going to come talk to the third graders, and that he wanted Becky and me to be there as well. She also told me that this was going to be low key, no media, just Tony talking with the class and trying to keep them positive after losing a special friend. A lot of the kids were having a tough time understanding why this would happen to one of their classmates. None of the kids knew about Tony's visit, so it was going to be a surprise.

I will never forget the day Tony came to talk to the class. Unfortunately, Becky wasn't able to make it. I arrived about a half hour early and met Linda Gallman at the back door of the school. She thought I should have some time to talk with Tony one on one, so she took me to an empty room where I could meet with him. A few minutes later Tony came in and immediately gave me a hug. I had about a half hour with him, talking about what had happened and telling him about the boys. I tried to especially tell him some things about Travis, so he'd have an idea what kind of boy he was, when talking to the class. He shared with me how he had dealt with his own son's death, gave me insightful advice about overcoming tragedy and acknowledged that men and women grieve differently. He also gave me an autographed picture of himself and wrote a personal note to Becky and me. The note said, *"To the Findleys: I know God still has great plans for your family. Trust Him to show this to you."* Under his name he wrote "Jeremiah 29:11," which says, *"For I know the plans I have for you," declares the LORD, "plans to prosper you and not to harm you, plans to give you hope and a future."*

We then went to the classroom where the third graders were. Tony was wonderful with them. He started out by asking who had watched the Super Bowl. Every hand shot up. Then he said, "You know, your friend Travis is doing alright, because he is up in heaven now with the Lord." He told them to think about and cherish all the great times they had had with Travis, because that is the way he would want them to remember him. I thought of Travis' bright smile, and how he wouldn't want his classmates to be sad but to keep laughing and having fun. That's the way Travis was. Tony also talked about his own son, and how he was thankful that he had him for nineteen years, and how he always thought of the good times. I think as the kids walked out of that class and that school on that day, they felt better about where Travis was.

After Tony was done, I was able to spend another fifteen minutes or so talking with him again. I can understand why the Colts players respect him so much. I didn't look at that meeting as a time with the coach of the Indianapolis Colts. I looked at it as spending time with a man of faith and a guy that I had something in common with because of unfortunate tragedies in our lives. He kept telling me to focus on the positive, and I will never forget that. He also gave me his phone number and told me to call anytime. And I will never forget that, either. Since then we have developed a friendship, and I will call him from time to time. If I leave him a voice mail he always gets back to me. His voice mails and calls really lift me up. He is an inspiration for me, and an example for all dads who have lost a child. He shows us that we can make it through even when we don't know how we are going to do it.

Tuesday mornings

We all need someone to help us make it through, and that is how the Tuesday morning Dads Group formed. This is a group of guys who get together because they need an

184

outlet—someone they can lean on, learn from, get advice from, cry with, laugh with, and have the commonality of being around other men who feel many of the same emotions after the tragedy of losing a child. Although we all have suffered through different tragedies, we share the same feelings and emotions.

Coming to this group, as I would immediately find out, was one of the most important and best decisions of my life. It helped the grieving process, because when tragedy strikes, you feel all alone in a great big world. Your world has stopped, but the outside world continues to move on at a frenzied pace, and you feel like it should all stop because of what you are personally going through. But it doesn't. So this group has helped me learn how to live with tragedy, because you can never "get over it" nor should you even try—and regardless, the world marches on.

When someone new comes to the group, everyone around the table spends time telling their "story." It can be unsettling and emotional. I've seen some of the dads really tear up and struggle through their story. Other dads pass altogether because they can't do it on that particular day. Whenever a dad starts to cry, whoever is next to him will always put a hand on his shoulder to comfort him, because he KNOWS what they are feeling. It is a pretty somber time, listening to all the stories that have affected men of all walks of life and professions. But it is necessary, because the deep connection helps us realize that we are not alone, and that others are feeling what we are feeling.

There are no rules in this group. Everyone can share their feelings however they want, and no one is judged negatively or considered less of a man or weak. And no one feels that their tragedy is worse than the others.

I have gotten some great advice from these men. Most of them had been through several years of grief when I first came to the group, while for others it was still fresh like mine. Sometimes we go around the group and share what we do on the special days, such as birthdays and holidays or the anniversary date of the death. I have learned that you should do whatever feels right for you at the time. Family members and friends will need to accept that you have to do things your own way with birthdays and holidays. There really is no time limit. The death of a child is forever. You don't "move on" or "get over it." No one has a clue about that unless they have been through it. No one. You basically have to learn to live "with" it. The pain never goes away, but it will lessen in time. Anniversary dates of the deaths of our children are extremely hard, even after several years.

All the guys in the Dads Group are only a phone call away if we need someone to talk to. E-mail is an easy tool to keep each other updated on things going on in our lives, or to say I need your thoughts and prayers about a hard day or a tough date coming up. We occasionally have social get-togethers with the wives or significant others. Sometimes some of the dads get together for lunch, or an outing to a baseball game. There is a comfort factor with this group, because each has walked in the others' shoes.

But this group doesn't sit around and feel sorry for each other because of unthinkable grief. We have learned that we can still live, and be productive members of society, and honor our children by living the best lives we can. Some days the mood is light and we can joke around and laugh a lot. And we need that. Other days the mood can be heavy, and the talk turns serious about what we are feeling or how we feel about a certain subject. Ultimately, we have a source of connection because of our situations, and can guide each other through the rough spots ... and rough spots can pop up at any time and be triggered by a multitude of things that remind us of our beloved children.

I encourage any man out there who has lost a child or children, to get the needed counseling, find or start a group like our Tuesday morning Dads Group, go to groups set up for parents who have lost a child—but no matter what, do something. The worst thing is to do nothing. Don't think you have to be Superman and handle it all on your own and be tough about it. Don't be afraid to admit what you are feeling, because you are not alone. If you go through the right avenues, you can find genuine, invaluable support from others who KNOW what you are going through and who "get it."

I want to close with what I know is my greatest source of comfort. That is the amazing grace of God and the hope we have through his son Jesus Christ. Without leaning on Him, I'm really not sure how I could have made it through this terrible loss in my life. Wherever I go, I give these words of advice

- Never take a single day for granted, NOT EVER.
- Live your life to the fullest and be the best person you can be in the process.
- Parents, love your kids with all your soul and make sure they know you love them.
- Believe that the only hope we have after our time on earth is to trust God, and that we will see our loved ones once again in heaven.

If there is any comfort in my tragedy of losing two children, it's the fact that Jake and Travis are together in heaven. They have always been together, and have always been best buds, so I am thankful that they are both with each other now in paradise.

Jake and Travis—

I love you both so much. My heart aches for you each and every day, but I have the hope that I KNOW I will see you both again one day.

I love you guys!!

Love,
Dad

Chuck Findley

Our Group Continues

EVERY TUESDAY MORNING AT 7:00 A.M., THOSE OF US WHO ARE A part of the Dads Group continue to gather around tables that have been grouped together in the coffee shop of the Hilton North Hotel (formerly the Omni) in Indianapolis, Indiana. Each of us is not sure how long we will continue to come. We just keep coming. And we keep thinking about the next dad who might be coming to join us.

From left to right: Steve Reed, Jerry Toomer, Marv Hamilton, Dave Toombs, Chuck Findley, Rick Larrison, Jerry Baker, Mike Laird, Jon Pavey, Mark Fritz, Adolf Hansen, Tom Harford, Jim Schroeder, Jim Runnels, Jim Dodds, Anthony Pokorny.

Your Group May Begin

IF YOU'RE A DAD WHO HAS LOST
A SON OR A DAUGHTER,

FIND ANOTHER DAD WHO HAS LOST
A SON OR A DAUGHTER

AND HAVE A CUP OF COFFEE.

IF YOU'RE NOT A DAD WHO HAS LOST
A SON OR A DAUGHTER,

AND YOU KNOW A DAD WHO HAS LOST
A SON OR A DAUGHTER,

SHARE THIS BOOK WITH HIM.

Resources Dads Have Found Helpful

WEB SITES

American Association of Suicidology
www.suicidology.org

Bereaved Parents
www.bereavedparentsusa.com

Brooke's Place for Grieving Young People and Families
www.brookesplace.org

Centering Corporation
www.centering.org

Compassionate Friends: Supporting a Family after a Child Dies
www.compassionatefriends.org

Death of a Child – Grief of the Parents
www.athealth.com/consumer/disorders/parentalgrief.html

Email Support Groups
www.griefnet.org

Families Helping Families
www.jdf-fhf.org

Lamenting Sons: Fathers and Grief
www.members.tripod.com/~LifeGard/index-4.html

Parents of Murdered Children
www.pomc.com

Substance Abuse Resources
www.substanceabusesupport.com

Survivors of Suicide
www.survivorsofsuicide.com

Tuesday Mornings with the Dads
www.tuesdayswiththedads.org

BOOKS

Thomas Attig. *How We Grieve: Relearning the World.* Oxford, 1996 – ISBN 019507456

David Fleming. *Noah's Rainbow: A Father's Emotional Journey from the Death of his Son to the Birth of his Daughter.* Baywood, 2006 – ISBN 0895033151

Thomas Golden. *Swallowed by a Snake: The gift of the Masculine Side of Healing.* Second edition. Golden Healing Publications, 2000 – ISBN 9780965464918

Adolf Hansen. *Responding to Loss: A Resource for Caregivers.* Baywood, 2004 – ISBN 0895033011

J. Shep Jeffreys. *Helping Grieving People: When Tears Are Not Enough.* Brunner-Routledge, 2005 – ISBN 0415946034

Dennis Klass. *The Spiritual Lives of Bereaved Parents.* Brunner/Mazel, 1999 – ISBN 0876309910

Dale Lund, ed. *Men Coping With Grief.* Baywood, 2000 – ISBN 0895032120

Kim Manlove. *Odyssey: Love, Loss, and Redemption.* Blurb, 2008 – ISBN 9780615300443

Terry Martin and Kenneth Doka. *Men Don't Cry…Women Do: Transcending Gender Stereotypes of Grief.* Brunner/Mazel, 2000 – ISBN 0876309953

James Miller and Thomas Golden. *When a Man Faces Grief – A Man You Know Is Grieving.* Willowgreen Publications, 1998 – ISBN 1885923274

Robert A. Neimeyer, ed. *Meaning Reconstruction and the Experience of Loss.* American Psychological Association, 2001 – ISBN 1557987424

Colin Murray Parkes. *Bereavement: Studies of Grief in Adult Life* (third edition). International Universities Press, 1998 – ISBN 0823604829

Jerre Petersen. *Heartworks – A Father's Grief.* Heart Work, 2003 – ISBN 0972937714

Therese Rando. *Treatment of Complicated Mourning.* Research Press, 1993 – ISBN 0878223290

Barbara Rosof. *The Worst Loss: How Families Heal from the Death of a Child.* Henry Holt. 1994 – ISBN 080503241X

Harriet Sarnoff Schiff. *The Bereaved Parent.* Penguin Books, 1977 – ISBN 0140050434

Mary A. White. *Harsh Grief, Gentle Hope.* NavPress, 1995 – ISBN 0891099085

Robert Wilkinson. *Love, Dad: Healing the Grief of Losing a Child.* AuthorHouse, 2002 – ISBN 0759645590

Barbara Wilson and Michael Wilson. *First Year, Worst Year: Coping with the Unexpected Death of Our Grown-up Daughter.* Wiley, 2004 – ISBN 9780470093597

Nicholas Wolterstorff. *Lament for a Son.* Eerdmans, 1987 – ISBN 9780802802941

LaVergne, TN USA
07 September 2009
157134LV00007B/179/P